VIEWABILITY

viewability

HARNESS THE POWER OF YOUTUBE ADS
AND BE THERE FOR YOUR CUSTOMER
—WHEN IT REALLY COUNTS

TOM BREEZE

LIONCREST
PUBLISHING

VIEWABILITY

Harness the Power of YouTube Ads and Be There
for Your Customer – When It Really Counts

ISBN   978-1-61961-685-1 *Paperback*
        978-1-61961-686-8 *Ebook*

For Kirsten and our sons, Milo and Inigo

Contents

Introduction

Thanks for dropping by, and well done. By showing up, you've signed on to learn one of the fastest, least-exploited, and most powerful and successful ways to build your customer base: creating YouTube videos exquisitely targeted to each customer's moment of need.

That concept's probably brand new to you. You're reading the first book ever on how to make an effective video ad for YouTube. No one has taught this stuff before. But you've doubtless heard superlatives such as "fastest" applied to various techniques, so you may be feeling a bit skeptical.

For the time being, keep an open mind; park preconceived ideas at the door. I'm asking you to consider advertising differently than you ever have before, even if you're a pro. But you're human, so you're likely to find yourself resisting—until you get your first results.

If you apply the techniques in this book, you can't help but get great results, because the techniques work. Most advertising goes wrong because it focuses on the wrong thing and starts with the business: "Here's my idea; here's my product; here's what it does." But to get in front of your potential customers, you've got to turn that around. Instead, start with the user. What are they looking for at this moment, and how can you help them?

I'm certainly not asking you to forget about return on investment (ROI): quite the opposite. Focusing on your customer instead of your business happens to be the best way to make money. In my agency, Viewability, we specialize in YouTube advertising and test everything to do with it. We prove the value of a customer-centered approach every day. My number-one priority for my clients and for myself is how much we're spending and how much we're getting back in return, and how quickly—this is how we've become Google's highest-spending agency worldwide on performance-based YouTube advertising campaigns.

By the way, this book focuses on YouTube because I believe it's the most powerful web platform, it offers tremendous opportunities to the few who know how to use it, and I know it inside and out. But the book's fundamental lessons apply to *any* advertising medium, whether online or offline. They're based on the psychology behind how people respond to advertising. These lessons represent no less than *the future of advertising*.

THE PSYCHOLOGICAL EDGE

Inspired by a determination to study what works, based on measuring the results, I've used my scientific background to hone the techniques I'm about to share with you. This book lays out both the theory and the methods, all grounded in principles of psychology and tested in the real world.

Psychology is the key to effective advertising: Connecting with the people who make up your potential audience—giving them a great experience by being useful—requires you to understand how they're thinking *at the moment they need you*. And studying human behavior is what psychology is all about. My background makes it easy for me to peek inside the minds of the potential customers of any type of business, and my aim is to do the same.

My fascination with how people think and react led me to study psychology. At the University of Leeds in the North of England, I learned many of the methods I use to test YouTube ads today. Paying part of my tuition with my online poker winnings, I became interested in the behavior of poker players in particular. I also noticed my own behavior: For example, when I was on a winning streak, I would start to take more risks and end up winning or losing big.

This interest led to my choice of gambling as the topic of my dissertation. I focused on roulette players, whose behavior is easier to measure than that of poker players, because they play against the table, not other players. One of the many behavioral factors my colleagues and I studied was the form of currency. We proved that when people used chips or online accounts, which are less tangible, they gambled more freely and lost more quickly than they did with cash.

Another industry reflects the influence of currency formats. As banks continue to move to digital technology, people's behavior around money has also changed—dramatically. So, it's no surprise so many people are in debt. We hardly ever hold money at all anymore; all we have are numbers on a screen, rather than cash in hand.

For my master's thesis in psychology, I moved from gambling behavior to sports performance. My colleagues and I taught golfers visualization and muscle-relaxation techniques, and they all improved their putting performance, some by quite a large margin.

When we worked with field-hockey goalkeepers, we learned how unaware people can be of their own behavior. We asked them where they tend to look when facing a penalty flick, and they all said they look at the ball or the player. Then we tracked their eye movements. The goalkeepers who saved the most penalties actually looked at the angle of the shooter's stick at the last moment. They had no idea they did that. So now we would advise looking at the stick, as opposed to the ball or players, which is generally what is taught.

Behavioral blindness is so common that comedians play it for laughs. It's funny when they mention an experience we all go through without really paying attention. In advertising, most people's lack of behavioral self-awareness correlates to their buying habits. When you ask people why they bought something, you'll often hear reasons that have nothing to do with what *actually* influenced them. Often the reason they give sounds right to them, and they believe it. But the data tells a different story.

Finding the stories in data is another skill I owe to my background. Psychology requires immersion in statistical analysis of populations and variables. Data is critical for perceiving causes and trends, so I became very comfortable looking at numbers and interpreting them. In the agency today, we base our client work on large amounts of data about how many people view videos and for how long, how many of them click and subscribe or buy, and how many don't.

EARLY ADS FAILED FAST

After I received my master's degree in 2008, I launched a business as a coach focusing on business performance. I used psychological approaches to help clients overcome anxiety and gain confidence in their presentations. I thought the best way to promote what I did was via the Yellow Pages. (Remember those? This was 2008!) I couldn't have been more wrong, and I spent a fortune for nothing.

I got much better results online, using Google AdWords, which I hadn't even heard of until I received an offer of £30 through the mail to spend on the advertising system. On day one of running my first ad, Google's £30 earned me a new client that paid £240, which seemed like a great return. As I kept spending money on AdWords, more potential customers called the office.

About a year later, I decided to shoot a video for my website. I knew nothing about creating videos and didn't have the equipment. I had no decent lighting, and I used my parents' old-school camcorder. It had such a terrible mic, though, that I had to use a lapel mic, plug it into a Dictaphone, and sync the audio with the video later. But that's not even the most embarrassing part. The video took me more than a hundred takes because I thought I had to do it all the way through every time.

When I look back on that video, I think it was terrible,

but it had good content, and it was one of the first videos on a website in the UK. So, the results weren't terrible: Overnight, that video more than tripled the number of people who wanted to do business with me. That's when I knew that video could really work, and it changed every aspect of my business.

THE BIG BREAKTHROUGH: VIDEO + ADVERTISING

I made more videos, in which I basically said to my potential customers, "Here's another quick tip to help you become a more confident presenter." After I gave the tip, I added, "If you fancy working with me, here are my details." The formula not only worked, it also inspired the next phase of my career. During a public-speaking workshop for business owners, a few attendees came up to me to say, "We love your videos. Can you show us how to do them?" "Yeah," I thought. "Sure, I can do that."

Soon I was creating videos for a variety of businesses. My partner at the time promoted the videos on YouTube, and we built an agency using search engine optimization (SEO)— using various strategies to raise the ranking of videos in Google search results, along with the videos' chances of being seen. We made sure our clients' videos appeared at the top of both YouTube and Google search results.

SEO worked well until Google and YouTube changed

the rules, but I was never an SEO fan. It felt like gaming the system. A top-ranking video doesn't compensate for useless content, and Google has always worked to deliver the most applicable results for each search. If you've got valuable content, people read it, talk about it, and share it, and *that's* what merits results. So, gaming the system by salting keywords was ruining the process for everyone; it ultimately doomed SEO.

When the SEO results stopped coming, I had a problem. Clients were not happy because they were no longer on the front pages of Google and YouTube; their lead generation was drying up. I had to do something fast. I experimented, going back to AdWords and spending my own money running one of my client's videos as an ad on YouTube. To my surprise (and utter relief!), the video earned him many more customers than SEO ever had. And it was cheaper, because I could do it all with just a computer and AdWords, not a big staff. Soon enough, I introduced all of our clients to YouTube advertising.

YOUTUBE'S MANY ADVANTAGES OVER EVERY OTHER PLATFORM

The word "cheap" no longer describes AdWords. When AdWords launched, it was possible to get a great deal because so few people were bidding for the space. As people found out that it generated amazing results, everyone wanted in. But space is limited on Google's front page; only the biggest companies can afford those few premium spots. One client, for example, pays sixty-five dollars per click on Google for some keywords, and it still turns a profit.

Like AdWords and Facebook, YouTube is also already getting more expensive. But what sets it apart from all other platforms is that the YouTube platform is *growing* as fast as the demand. As more and more videos are created and uploaded every second, this growth gives advertisers more space to advertise. As I write, something like *300 hours of videos are uploaded every single minute*, and that number continues to grow. On Facebook, advertisers are fighting to appear in your news feed, which is like one small Main Street where everyone is trying to buy a billboard. YouTube is, in effect, building a whole new Main Street every day.

A major psychological benefit of advertising on YouTube is that the platform is more like Google than like Facebook. With Facebook, people typically check their feed because they're bored, waiting in line, or wanting to connect with friends—it's like a social party. And *at* a party, you're unlikely to win friends if you intrude on people with an irrelevant message, such as "Hey, look at this great new stuff I've got." No one likes that.

YouTube and Google are more like libraries: People go

there looking for specific information. So, if you get in front of an audience on YouTube with a helpful message, you can start a relationship, then transition naturally into that next conversation: "If you want to find out more, I've got this great thing that's going to help you." When that relationship begins, it's much easier to sell, as long as you continue to be classy about it, not salesy.

Being British, I tend to be quite reserved. The fact that selling doesn't necessarily come naturally to me is an asset on YouTube, where people don't want a strong sales pitch. If you insist on putting the hard sell in front of people there, you'll only annoy them.

A wise Uber driver lent insight to this discussion on the way to the San Antonio airport after he asked what I do for a living. Normally that conversation ends with, "So you're that guy who runs those annoying ads I can't skip on YouTube." However, he told me that he doesn't mind ads on YouTube because going there feels like going to a website built by others where he can learn or be entertained. He said he really hates ads on Facebook, where, "it's as if I've built my own home for my family and friends." He said he sees the ads there as invading his personal space.

Whether your customers see Facebook as their online home, a party, or a party in their home, they may not want to see your ads there, and they're certainly not looking for you. And whether they see YouTube as a library or some other space, they *are* looking for you there. *Every single day YouTube attracts about five billion views.*

These views represent a whole lot of people who want to know, do, or buy something, or who want to be inspired. Your job is to find out what they want and give it to them. As you do, you will find out more about them: demographic data—gender, age, location, household income, parental status, and so on—as well as their search behavior, interests, and their position in the buying cycle.

YouTube makes it simple to do that type of testing. We can learn so much so quickly about how large numbers of people actually behave and buy. These aren't university students paid to turn up for a psychological experiment, as in most scientific studies.

Many studies about research show that as soon as people know they're being watched, they change their behavior. They want to be good and helpful, so they work harder. In the gambling experiments that I carried out for my dissertation and thesis, for example, there's little question that participants modified their observed behavior—in ways that were difficult to measure.

With YouTube, we're testing the authentic buying behavior of real people in their everyday lives, and we can track all this information. We get incredibly valuable data while we're making sales.

THE MAGIC OF VIDEO, BACKED BY SCIENCE

At this moment, you're in exactly the right place to learn how to be useful for your customers using YouTube advertising. If you don't, you'll be like everyone else—putting out promotions the way you always have and wondering why you're getting the same weak results.

This is also exactly the right time. YouTube is still under many advertisers' radars because they don't realize its impact. Or maybe they tried an ad there and got poor results because they didn't know what they were doing. They didn't have this book. That means you could be the first in your business category to connect with your customers in this powerful way. No other platform beats the connection you can have with your customers on YouTube. They can get to know and trust you in seconds. The medium of video enables this level of relationship building.

Video engages the brain and the senses more than a billboard, an image, or text does, because video offers a complete experience. If you think back to your childhood, you can probably remember at least one TV ad so vividly you can play it back in your head. But you rarely get that from a still-image or text ad.

For me, that TV commercial was "the red car and the blue car had a race," an animated musical ad for Milky Way chocolate bars. For my parents and grandparents, it was the Fairy Liquid ads. Every time they heard the name, they felt compelled to sing the same jingle they had heard when they were kids. Video is that sticky.

Video is also that attractive. We know that people, in huge numbers, seek out videos for information and inspiration at different moments in their lives. It's a safe bet you do, too.

That's not to say everyone heads over to YouTube. People use a variety of tactics in a variety of situations. Yet many types of searches particularly lend themselves to videos—tutorials or how-to, for example. The way a how-to video demonstrates a procedure provides the next-best thing to a classroom or other in-person experience. In fact, providing an experience is what video does best. People also love videos that review and compare products. You process video very differently than you process text. It's a much richer experience, which is what makes it so powerful.

Let's say you have a new board game that you don't know how to play. Reading the instructions may not help very much. Neither does having someone read the instructions to you. If someone plays the game in front of you, though, you'll quickly understand. (Maybe more board games should come with video instructions.)

Video also feeds our cravings. Imagine you're in the market for a car. Text alone won't cut it; everyone's text looks similar before it's read. If you *do* decide to read a car ad, the author will need to be a fabulous writer to make you feel the emotion of owning and driving a car.

At the very least, you want to see what the car looks like, what colors it comes in, and what's under the hood. So, a photo is better than text alone. But you really want to know what the car *feels* like—how it actually runs, how everything works. Of course, then what you want is to go and drive the damn thing, and that's the next step in the process. With video, you're as close as you can be without breathing in that new-car smell. It's a much more powerful sensory experience. Video holds tremendous power to trigger emotions, and our emotions lead to purchasing decisions. And a YouTube video can include a link that will take a viewer to a website to book a test-drive.

HOW TO WORK WITH THIS BOOK

This isn't a book that makes sense to skip through. I've set it up the way I set up a video: to tell a story in sequence, step by step. Each section builds on the one that came before.

When I read a business book, I love it when I can follow a thought process throughout, without having to write anything down. Each chapter gives me something to think about and a sense of completion. I can tick each one off and be inspired to move on to the next. I want you to have that experience as well.

It's a logical progression, perhaps also inspired by the Game Boy I played with as a kid. I would have to beat the big boss at the end of each level. As soon as I did, I reached the next level and felt as though I had achieved something. I could put down the toy at each stopping point if I wanted, for as long as I wanted, and bask in my success.

So, read the chapters through once in sequence, as you would watch a video. Go at your own pace. Then, as you work on a project, you can return to whatever chapter inspires you at the moment.

The book's chapters lay out these moments in sequence:

1. The Moments We Live In: Missed Opportunities from the Audience's Perspective
2. The Moments of Truth: Converting Viewers into Customers
3. Mapping Your Customer's Moments: How to Find Those Opportunities
4. The Message for the Moment: How to Define It
5. Meeting the Moment: The Logistics of Making It Happen

Congratulations! You've just beaten the first big boss. Feel free to bask in your success. Have a cup of tea, a glass of wine, or even champagne, and when you're ready, let's move on to Level 1...sorry, Chapter 1.

The Moments We Live In: Missed Opportunities from the Audience's Perspective

Moments of need occur every day in the lives of your potential audience members. For example, someone is getting married, going on vacation, or finding out that she's pregnant. Every time a person searches a mobile device or a computer with intent to find information or inspiration, *that* is a moment. People have many moments every single day, and each moment is an advertising opportunity for a brand or company. As you look at all the moments when your audience members need you, ask yourself whether you're there for them in a meaningful way. Probably not, I'm betting, because so few brands are.

For example, in December 2015, I decided to train for the London Marathon. After a freak accident killed one of my best friends, the hundreds of people who loved Pete formed a charity in his memory. Another close friend was training for the marathon to support that charity, until an injury forced him to drop out. So, on the spur of the moment, in front of all my friends in our WhatsApp group, and without ever having run a marathon, I committed to run in his place—a decision I rapidly regretted.

I went directly to Google and innocently typed "how to run a marathon." The first thing I found was this sobering advice: "Do not attempt to run a marathon unless you have twenty-five weeks to train." Right. At the sixteen-week point, I was already way behind, and I realized I knew nothing about what I had taken on.

I began frantically searching websites for anything helpful, and before long I found YouTube videos uploaded by marathon runners. Meanwhile, all of these questions flooded into my head, such as "What shoes should I buy? What clothing do I need? How do I get fit? What should I eat?" There were many other questions I didn't even know to ask at that point: "Where can I find a trainer and a physiotherapist? How do I join a running club and locate a hotel near the starting line?"

I was in a moment—my marathon moment; I was hungry

for information, but advertisers let me down. They didn't *help* me. I can't understand why I didn't see ads for Nike or other shoe brands, for hotels, or for the other things I needed. All these brands that could've won my business weren't getting in front of me.

In case you're wondering, brands have not gotten much wiser in the fifteen months since I launched my marathon search. Moments ago, I typed "marathon training" into YouTube. The ad that came up first was a day in the life of some volleyball players. I have no idea what that's promoting. I can't see any relevant ads running on most of the video choices—nothing that would be helpful if I were starting my research today. It's crazy; we're talking about the third-most visited site in the world and the second-largest search engine.

This craziness is true in the case of every brand and every moment for every customer. Very few people are advertising effectively on YouTube. You might see a Nike ad to launch a new clothing line plastered over the front of YouTube, but when you search for information about running a marathon, you see random ads that aren't addressing your needs in the moment. It's not as if these brands don't know that marathon beginners exist. The brands are simply missing those moments.

DOING THE NUMBERS

They're not alone. According to Google, brands—including those like yours—miss the moments when their customers are searching for them *nine times out of ten.* As an advertiser, you can be sure your customers are searching for you at this moment. Almost 50 percent of internet users look for products online before going to a store; people stay on YouTube on their phones or tablets an average of forty minutes at a time; and, it bears repeating, *YouTube gets five billion views a day.* You're missing a huge opportunity to be there for all of the people who need your help.

Where are all the brands? They're spending fortunes on TV advertising. If they're on YouTube at all, they treat it as an afterthought, despite its many advantages. As more proof of how crazy this all is, here's another stunning Google stat for you: *Purchasing intent is 150 percent higher on YouTube than on TV.*

So where *are* you when your customers need you?

As one more example of so many missed opportunities, let's return to the marathon example. It's not news to physiotherapists that people training for marathons often get injured. These professionals should have been there for me as soon as I decided to search for how to run a marathon. Some practitioner should have connected with me in a video offering compassionate advice. For example, "To avoid injury as you train for your marathon, don't forget to stretch. Let me give you these three techniques that will help you."

Not only would I have watched that video, but I also would have felt grateful and even a little indebted to this helpful person. I would've been wide open to the follow-up message: "If you ever want to come and see us, we're offering a free marathon-prep session" or whatever the offer might be. "Then you can get to know us, and we can give you more advice about your marathon." Sold.

When I did feel my muscles tightening up, I searched for a physiotherapist ("physio in Reigate," where I live) and saw lots of ads competing for space. Every one of these advertisers had missed out on developing a relationship when I searched for how to run a marathon.

These moments that brands ignore are great for us as an agency, because we can tap into them very cost-effectively. But I'm sharing a lot of what we practice in the hopes of reducing the number of random or annoying ads on YouTube. These types of ads give viewers a poor experience, and it doesn't have to be that way. We all have the opportunity, even the responsibility, to build a more useful platform.

MOMENTS ALONG THE PATH TO PURCHASE

These moments in your customers' lives reflect different natural levels of urgency. In my marathon moment, for example, shoes were an immediate need. During that moment, if I had seen an article praising a certain type of running shoe, I would have bought a pair on the spot. For less-urgent needs, such as a nutrition plan, I would have taken more time to shop around. At the time, hotels weren't even on my list.

For every product or service, there are people who are ready to buy now, those who are doing research, and those who are slightly interested. These three different types of customers require three different approaches. If you have a brick-and-mortar store, you already know these people: You find the buy-now people at the checkout counter, the researchers in the store asking questions, and the mildly interested folks window-shopping.

In my marathon moment, I modeled the behavior of all three types of customers at various points in my process. Advertisers needed to speak to me differently, depending on where I stood on the path toward purchasing each product or service. To shed more light on the path to purchase, let's return to the brick-and-mortar-store analogy.

When I'm walking past the store, I may stop and look

in the window. I may even go inside the store if I see a product or feature I like.

When I'm in the store, I need you to give me advice and demonstrate features that will interest me.

When I'm at the checkout counter with credit card in hand, I probably need only reassurance that I'm making the right decision.

Although customers need different approaches at different times, many brands advertise with just one message—one video—as if YouTube were TV. Most people watching, though, will see that one-size-fits-all video as nothing more than another irrelevant, repetitive ad. It's not a good user experience.

Understanding a person's position on the path to purchase is only one of many methods we can use to locate customers, but it's a valuable place to start. For example, let's look at two of the three positions on the path to purchase in my marathon example.

If a running-shoe brand knows I'm ready to buy, the message can be: "This is the best marathon shoe out there. Take it from the people who run in them. It's the one to buy if you're serious about running the marathon." That would've worked for me.

But a similar approach wouldn't have worked for my hotel on that same day because I wasn't ready to book a room yet. So, the brand would need a message more like this: "Here's something I'll bet you didn't know: Of all the things you've got to set up before your marathon, there's one thing that often gets put off until it's too late. That's your hotel."

Let's travel the path to purchase with another example: Imagine that you're selling vacations to Bermuda. The window-shopper in this example isn't searching but loves vacations with sea, sun, and sand. The in-store person is actively searching for a beach destination. The checkout customer has decided to go to Bermuda; for them, the questions switch to considerations such as "Which airline?" and "Where should I stay?"

BEING THERE DOESN'T ALWAYS MEAN GETTING IT RIGHT

Avoiding YouTube's wealth of opportunities isn't the only way brands fail. YouTube advertisers can miss the mark. Take this scenario that I experienced only this week: Much too early in the morning, my wife's and my two-year-old son jumped onto our bed to demand his favorite program: "Peppa Pig! Peppa Pig!" In self-defense, I grabbed my phone and found an episode on YouTube.

While the video was loading and before I handed the

phone to my impatient tot, I engaged iPhone's "Guided Access" feature, so he couldn't press other buttons on the phone. Using that feature also meant that I couldn't stop the ad—for a fabric softener in the UK—that showed up before the video.

Bear in mind that the moment occurred in the middle of winter, so it was freezing cold, and, at four forty-five in the morning, it was pitch-black outside. The video showed a half-naked lady in bed at midday. She was talking in a French accent about how beautiful it was to have the whole soft bed to herself. As my kid continued to shout "Peppa Pig!" I was thinking, "This is the total opposite of the experience I'm having right now." It was a frustrating moment.

The company was getting its product in front of me at exactly the wrong time with exactly the wrong branding. The only people looking for *Peppa Pig* at that hour are in no mood to watch those kinds of ads. If the brand wants to target parents, it should know that the only message we'll tolerate at that hour might be advice on how to get our kids to sleep longer or how to entertain them.

The experience had a powerful emotional impact. Because videos are that sticky, I may always remember it—but for all the wrong reasons. I get annoyed whenever I see the brand, which means I won't buy it. (Well, maybe I should say I don't *intend* to buy it. Remember, there's often a difference between what we *say* we'll do and what we *actually* do.)

WHY YOU'RE NOT ALREADY THERE

One reason advertisers haven't flocked to YouTube may be its youth. It was born only in 2005, Google bought it the following year, and it introduced advertising in 2007. It has grown to thirteen times the size of all other video platforms combined, but few people know what to do with it and how to do it because they still haven't done it. As an agency, we had to learn everything we know by trial and error, using psychology, tracking, and investing to see what works.

We know, for example, that advertisers who simply transfer their TV ads to YouTube are likely to be disappointed in the results. TV-to-YouTube transfers often take place when brands spend up to hundreds of thousands on those TV campaigns and have them approved. The one-size-fits-all approach *can* work on TV, especially for big brands. They're playing the long game, building brand awareness. They wouldn't *be* big brands unless their approach was working for them.

But that approach is far from the best use of YouTube, a platform that thrives on customized messages and whose viewers demand a personal experience. When your goal is to be useful to people, you'll create videos they love and that attract high-quality customers.

Some advertisers have also failed to take YouTube seriously because it's "apparently" full of babies and kittens. And there has been a widespread misconception that YouTube plays second fiddle to Facebook and TV. But that's changing. As soon as our clients get better results from YouTube than from Facebook or TV, they see it as the serious, valuable platform it is.

Another criticism of YouTube—the unskippable thirty-second ads that viewers have to sit through before they can watch their video of choice—is about to expire (as I write this). YouTube announced that it would end the practice in 2018. That's great news for the users, so it's also great news for you.

WHEN SCIENCE AND ART DON'T COMMUNICATE

Still another reason you're not doing YouTube ads might be the opinion of your creative director. In meetings with brands that want to build YouTube ads, I've often noticed a similar reaction. Some creative people don't like that I can track everything. They don't want to see the numbers, especially when the numbers conflict with their preconceptions. When they say, "That's just numbers," I gently remind them that the numbers represent people.

Ironically, these creative folks sometimes get stuck in their ways. They know how TV works, and they're used to its rules. But they can be reluctant to learn or be bound by the rules of YouTube, the new kid on the block.

Also, because some creative-team members are so used to TV processes, they expect to just create ads and hand them off to production. But that silo approach doesn't work for YouTube, where quality demands teamwork.

The problem gets even worse with the people who want to make one ad for TV and apply it to YouTube, instead of taking advantage of the platform's strengths. YouTube lets you create multiple ads, one for each type of audience member, and do so simply and inexpensively.

Don't get me wrong: Creativity is important; it can go a long way toward helping a video stick in the viewer's mind. But when art and science collide in a meeting, it's best to allow art to influence and science to guide the process. An ad's priority has to be turning its cost into profit.

HOW TO TURN AD COST INTO PROFIT: START WITH THE USER

Even the YouTube-shy will come around eventually as they see brands around them succeed. If they try the platform themselves, they will reinforce their belief in its power. A proven system for success is to start with the user, and YouTube enables that. It allows you to create different ads to help different people, based on what they're seeking.

Creating a really good experience for your customer just happens to be the best strategy for return on investment. Part of my brain is always thinking about ROI. In fact, I believe in it so much that my agency only gets paid when we get results. Clients climb onboard quickly because I take all the risk, they know I'll spend every waking hour working for them, and they won't have to pay for that time. This way, it feels more like a partnership in which my clients and I grow together.

Helping advertisers to attract more customers would be financial value enough, but YouTube doesn't stop there. It rewards engaging ads by lowering the cost and offering more reach. YouTube can afford to be that generous because they benefit when the users have a great experience and, in turn, engage with more ads.

DIFFERENT METRICS APPLY TO ONLINE ADS THAN TO TV

When it comes to TV advertising, the concepts of reach—how many people have seen the ad—and frequency—how many times—aren't all they're cracked up to be. But they're basically all TV advertising can show for itself. Actually, TV advertisers also look at the programs, channels, and times that their ads run. But the fact that an ad ran, for example, forty times in a week doesn't mean that the frequency caused people to buy the brand, *and* the advertisers can't easily track whether it did.

Even worse, it's not uncommon for brands to spend *more* money on advertising and see a *reduction* in sales.

Compare all that with online advertising, where you can track literally every impression, view, and click, and then turn on a dime. Reach and frequency are simple. You can get in front of masses of people if you want, as frequently as you want. Or you might find you want to limit frequency so you don't bombard your audience with the same ad.

In fact, it often makes sense to limit the number of times you show any ad to just once. For example, our agency invented and often uses a method called the "Cascading Campaign." As soon as one viewer sees one video ad without actually acting on it, we'll follow up with a new one. After they see the second ad, we'll follow up with a third. They get an amazing user experience for two reasons: They never see the same ad twice, and we can control the flow through all three ads and even tell a story.

GETTING PEOPLE ENGAGED

So, if you happen to want reach and frequency, you can have them on YouTube and other online platforms. The tough part—online or off—tends to be getting people to engage with your ads. But remember, people go to YouTube with the intention of watching a video to find information. Put a useful and relevant video ad in front of them, and they'll watch it. That's what they came for.

With TV, on the other hand, most people fast-forward through commercials or use the time to get a coffee. They're in a passive TV-viewing mode, not in an active information-searching mode.

That's not to suggest we humans love the ads that run before the YouTube videos we came to watch. But we experience them differently than we do TV ads. Even when we can't skip them quickly or at all, we rarely walk away from them. We'll wait for the video because we're on one of four missions—to be inspired, to learn, to buy, or to do something. Every one of those missions means we're engaged.

HOW YOUTUBE PERFECTS THE CONTENT CREATOR–ADVERTISER RELATIONSHIP

How's this for engagement? If you've found a good niche, you could easily get a million views on YouTube. And those numbers aren't even considered "viral" anymore.

The YouTube ecosystem tends to work like this: To set up ads, I spend money with AdWords. The amount of competition in the marketplace determines how much I spend per view, which typically ranges from two to twenty cents.

Up until recently, YouTube would take 45 percent of the revenue, and the content creator (the owner of the video that your ad precedes) would receive 55 percent. So, for example, that revenue-distribution formula meant that a 10-cent view would earn YouTube 4.5 cents and the content creator 5.5 cents.

However, more recently these payouts have changed and now the amount content creators get paid has been termed CPM, or cost per one thousand ad views. The vast majority of YouTubers earn anywhere between $0.30 and $2.50 CPM, with only the most popular channels earning around $10 CPM.

Everyone wins with this arrangement: YouTube gets financed to build a better website; content creators are paid for their efforts and will continue to create more and better videos for YouTube; advertisers cost-effectively get in front of the audience they seek; and users get a great experience.

By the way, you might have calculated that a million views at only three cents apiece still costs $30,000. But compare that with the cost of a typical TV ad, which, again, you can't target or sell nearly as well, or accurately track. Then consider how few purchases it'll take to more than pay for those YouTube views. Also keep in mind that the goal is return on investment (ROI). If I had to pay as much as one hundred dollars per view and it would still turn into profit, I would do it.

In terms of ROI, YouTube brings another edge over TV—a clickable link to the website. With TV, even if the viewer loves the ad, they don't have an easy, quick way to engage further with the brand. To continue the experience, they would have to log on to their mobile phone and search for the company. YouTube, on the other hand, makes the experience seamless and instantaneous, as in the following example.

A client who trains consultants wrote a book that he typically sells through the usual channels. At the beginning of his YouTube video, he says, "Here's a quick way to bring more consulting clients to your business." Then he presents three tips from one of his chapters. Viewers are engaged because they receive valuable information they can use right away. Should they decide to buy the book, they can simply click the link inside the video.

It helps if, at the end of the video, you make the ability to "buy now" clear to the viewer. For example, you could say,

"If you like these three tips, which are a tiny fraction of my book, you'll find much more in it about how to build your business, get clients, and close more deals. Click the link and buy the book right now." With TV, you need to tell the viewer what to do next, that is, call this number or visit this website. That's not so easy, and *making* it easy is a huge part of any effective sales effort.

INSIGHTS FROM THE OFFLINE WORLD

The most respected and successful advertisers play by this truth: The best way to communicate with your client online is to reflect an offline experience. Build an online world that feels human—that is more about being helpful and less about clicking links and signing up.

We can look to pre-internet days for inspiration. First, let's look at some historical basics. In describing customers' engagement with brands, advertisers and marketers have traditionally pointed to two "moments of truth":

- Whether customers decide to buy your product or another one in the first place
- Whether they decide to keep buying it after they try it

The moments-of-truth concept still applies to most products and services. Advertisers have always worked hard to influence the first moment by increasing motivation and ease of purchase. TV, radio, and print—basically the only pre-internet means of advertising—imposed a gap between the message and the point of sale. So, the in-store experience, which was often a store rep's helpful and personalized advice, had to pick up the slack. Influencing the second moment requires making sure the customer enjoys using the product.

As methods of influence have drastically changed, so have some of the concepts that guide them. Now advertisers speak of a "search moment" (also known as a "zero moment of truth," or "ZMOT" for short). People shopping for, say, a TV can go directly online to search product or service options and reviews. And they can buy on the spot—no more gaps.

Of course, just because shoppers *can* buy on the spot doesn't mean they *do*. They face an overwhelming number of choices. They'll do a lot of research before a significant purchase like a TV. They want to compare prices, get the best deal, and read reviews. If you're selling TVs, or furniture to put them on, or cable channels, these shoppers could use your help. Your YouTube ads can provide that help by talking to shoppers as though they're offline, face-to-face with you. Imagine they're in your office or store or, better yet, that you're a friend or neighbor sharing useful advice over a back fence or a cup of coffee.

YouTube enables that neighborly experience more realistically than anywhere else, except really in person. To reinforce the feeling of a personal conversation as you create your videos, remind yourself that you're talking to one person at a time, not to millions of people.

TAP INTO GOOGLE TO FIND YOUR AUDIENCE

Your customers are already out there. They're already using YouTube, and they're waiting for you. And Google, which has been tracking their interests and behavior since day one, is waiting to tell you about them—things like where they're going, what they're doing, how long they're staying, and how they're different from one another.

Google tracks everything. Its ability to collect and analyze user behavior has become so powerful that you can start building your audience with Google data alone. For example, Google's appropriately named "Similar Audiences" feature can analyze your uploaded email database and build you an audience ten times as big. That's an audience of only the people who are most likely to want to interact with your ads.

Google's artificial intelligence is getting more sophisticated all the time. In fact, soon when you tell Google you want to advertise a product, *it will find you customers.*

For now, though, you'll need to come up with your own

opportunities. In Chapter 2, you'll gain insight into what your customers really want from you and when they want it.

The Moments of Truth: Converting Viewers into Customers

Now that you've looked at where potential customers are on the path to purchase and what they're thinking, you're almost ready to take on this chapter's mission: inspiration to help you position your product or service in the best possible way. First, you need to make sure you're promoting something that *can* sell. When you do, this book will help your customers find it. Once they find, try, and love it, the experience sets off a chain reaction: they buy again, they trust the company enough to try its other offerings, and they tell their friends.

Start by answering advertising's two biggest yet most basic questions:

- When people come into your "store," do they become your customers?
- Do they end up becoming your lifelong customers?

Within those key questions are four more, each representing a moment of truth—search, purchase, reflection, and influence—that make up the entire customer experience. You need to perfect them all.

THE FOUR MOMENTS: SEARCH, PURCHASE, REFLECTION, AND INFLUENCE

With the internet came a new moment—**search: Will customers find you?** For companies, the search moment transformed everything. It didn't take long for people who went online to research and compare a product to also start buying online. Companies either adapted or went out of business. Of the four moments of truth, search is the one with which most of our clients come in needing our help. It's the moment I focus on in this book.

When customers get to the **purchase** phase, the question becomes **Will customers buy from you?** A big part of its answer lies in additional questions that we'll explore in this chapter.

The next moment is **reflection: Will customers think fondly of you?** I'll explain it by asking you to step back for a moment into the shoes of the consumer. Once you've bought something and taken it into your home, you trigger a second moment of truth: when you reflect upon that purchase. Do you like it? For example, when you've just bought a TV, there's that excitement around it. Someone puts it up on the wall, and either you're happy with how it looks or you're not. Then you play around with the controls until they become easy or they continue to feel unintuitive. At that point, upon reflection, you might either pronounce the purchase good or feel buyer's remorse.

Now slip your *advertiser* shoes back on: If you're the seller of that TV, you can and should support the crucial moment of reflection. For example, you could provide instruction in the form of a free support line for the first fourteen days. For some of our clients, these reflection-targeted campaigns have worked well. As soon as customers purchase online, they see more ads thanking them for buying, hoping they enjoy the product, and saying, "If you have any questions, let us know. Here are our contact details." These sorts of "thank-you campaigns," as my agency calls them, show that the advertiser is still working to be useful and positive.

Another big reason to make sure your customers are happy reflectors is because the next moment—**Influence: Will customers tell their friends about you?**—follows closely on the heels of reflection. Influence is the moment when someone notices the new TV and asks how its owner likes it. The influence moment can also inspire or direct a purchase, and that's the traditional, but limited, form of influence. Customers exert a far broader and more powerful scope of influence through what's known as "word of mouse": online reviews and comments, most often about either extreme of the satisfaction scale.

THREE FACTORS IN BUILDING THE RIGHT OFFER: PERCEIVED VALUE, MEANINGFUL BUSINESS REFLECTION, AND DESIRABILITY WITH EASE

As I mentioned, your ability to perfect the four moments of truth depends heavily on the attractiveness of your offer. That attractiveness, in turn, depends on these three factors.

1. PERCEIVED VALUE

Your customer needs to perceive your offer as useful and valuable, which can affect the choice between a freebie and a paid offer (among other things). If you're considering promoting a free offer, for example, also consider whether viewers will find it worthwhile. They may view some offers without cost as being without worth. In those cases, simply attaching even a nominal price can raise the perception of value.

Other offers, on the other hand, seem so intrinsically

valuable that customers welcome them even without forking over payment. A book by an established author tends to fall into the intrinsic-value category, even if it's free except for shipping and handling.

Another way to handle the free-versus-paid decision is to think of a free offer as a temporary fix. Many years ago, marketer James Lavers shared a clever analogy that has stayed with me: Imagine that customers come to your website with a headache. They receive your website's version of a free pill, which relieves them.

That pill was never meant to be a permanent solution, though, so when pain inevitably returns, customers come back for another dose. Don't fill *that* prescription, because the initial treatment earned you the right to try to deepen the relationship on the second visit. You might say something like, "To really help yourself out with your migraines, you can't keep taking these pills. You need a longer-term approach. Do you want to chat about that?" The once-relieved customers will be likely to take the next step because you've gained their trust.

2. MEANINGFUL BUSINESS REFLECTION

A second factor in your offer choice is this: Usefulness alone is not enough. To emotionally link the customer to you and your business, the offer must do even more than focus on the customer. It must also logically and memorably reflect on you, your business, and your unique style. The tricky part is that it must do so without seeming to focus on the business *at the expense of* the customer.

So, that physiotherapist I mentioned earlier would be wise to give free stretching tips while showing off their unique and effective methods. The ad's aim should be to launch a relationship by promoting the work of that one physiotherapist, not *all* physiotherapists.

My best advice, then, is don't copy others. In fact, consider doing the *opposite* of what your competitors are doing. That advice stands even if what they're doing seems successful.

What's more, don't underestimate the attention-getting power of breaking the mold. Some of the best marketing campaigns *are* the best because they've never been seen before, so they're unexpected.

On our agency's website, for example, we take the (at least *unusual*) approach of questioning whether YouTube ads will even work for visitors. I ask them to answer our three-question self-discovery tool,[1] to which I respond

---

1   At our agency, we use the term "self-discovery tool" instead of "survey" for a strategic reason: The purpose of a survey is often to help advertisers get what they want from customers. By contrast, our tool aims to help website visitors find what they want from us. It acts like a salesperson helping customers during a face-to-face interaction in a store.

with their results in one of eight videos. The videos help you identify what type of customers you might have on YouTube, how to get in front of them, and what ads to use. I'm also brutally honest about whether YouTube ads are worth pursuing for your company.

You also might find, as we have, that one offer isn't enough. The people whose answers have placed them among the agency candidates and who want to learn more can choose between "Join us at our exclusive training workshop, or order one of our strategy audits, known as a 'MAP Session.'"

3. DESIRABILITY WITH EASE

To help you pin down the right offer to test, make sure people actually want it, customize it to them, and make it easy for them to accept. In fact, in the vast majority of cases, time spent making things easy for customers is better than time spent on improving sales copy.

No matter what people seek when they go on YouTube, ease is what they *really* want. Make them happy by triggering thoughts like, "This is exactly what I was looking for, and it was easy; I bought it. Done." That's the type of buying experience that people have come to expect from services such as PayPal, Apple Pay, and Amazon. They tap a phone today, and tomorrow they receive their purchases. And if it's a digital product, they tap and want immediate access.

Consumers are becoming more and more demanding, and business owners have been slow to catch up with those demands. But you had better do so quickly or you'll lose customers. Even motivated buyers are likely to walk away if you make them jump through too many hoops.

Our agency's advertising sells so many products and services because we think about how we want to be treated and how we want to buy something. We make it easy to take the next step—signing up, getting something free, or buying—and so should you.

I'm thinking about a travel agency that earned my long-term business by offering exactly what I wanted: the ability to travel without having to arrange it. Every travel agency offers that service, of course, but this one made itself more appealing by showing it would help me without requiring me to sign up and present my entire itinerary at the door. I valued that experience because I didn't expect it (especially in the UK, where customer service tends to be terrible). In only two short calls, everything was booked!

To replicate that ease, consider how quickly you can take the customer offline or at least offer the option. Even if you greet them with a form, you might say, "Fill it in, if you like, to (reach a fill-in-the-blank goal). But if you don't like forms, just give us a call at ___."

Sure, you'll have to pay someone to answer that call, and you'll have to work harder to keep track of things offline that Google handles online. But sometimes a human just wants to speak to a human. For some transactions, customers might find human interaction to be essential, so listen to whether yours do. You may have to invest a little to become the brand with the best customer experience, but doing so nearly always pays for itself in the long run.

Making things easy for your customer might also work for you in the short term. For example, our agency has streamlined the client-onboarding process. We used to send out a series of emails, each containing forms for completion. No one liked that cumbersome system, so we changed it. Now we email new clients only a list of the needed information with a suggestion to give us a call when they're ready. We do everything at once, on the phone, in a personal way that deepens the relationship. The call also pleases clients, because it lets us get started that much sooner on meeting their goals.

THE PERFECT TRIANGLE CURES HEADACHES

Harness all three factors—value, reflection on your style,

and desirability with ease—by combining your business model with your analysis of the shopper's buying readiness.

Examples of offers that combine those traits can include webinars, documentaries, how-to videos, online tools, or books (the whole text or a chapter). For a consulting client, our agency targets interested viewers, then sends them to sign up for the client's book at only the cost of postage. If they don't go all the way to inputting their credit-card number and making the purchase, we'll target them with more follow-up remarketing video ads with further content and additional reasons why they should buy the book, along with the link to buy.

TO ATTRACT, ASK

To ensure that you build the right offer from all three factors, it's often easiest to ask your potential customers questions first before pitching your offers. Business consultant Perry Marshall inspired the self-discovery tool on my agency's website with ten-question surveys on his.[2] Those surveys include "Is Google AdWords for Me?" and "Is Facebook for Me?" When you fill out the survey, you're directed to his advice on how the platform would work for your advertising.

A word about pronouns: Where Marshall asks whether

2　"Free Tools," Perry Marshall, https://www.perrymarshall.com/marketing/tools/

something is right for "me," I would always phrase it as "you," because the second person seems more direct. I've yet to test my theory, but a study by Dan Golden, cofounder of Be Found Online, showed this: Saying "you" in the first six seconds of a video resulted in 60 percent more engagement for the rest of the video. The results held true across industries.

Inspired by Marshall's approach and informed by Golden's research, I decided to tailor my response to audience responses by video. Ryan Levesque's "Ask Method" helped me with this goal. His book discusses the marketing justification and strategy of various types of questions.

Levesque also recommends asking only one question on each page. This approach gives the respondent the impression of less work, along with early investment in the process. The method also encourages early investment with the suggestion to put the simplest questions (such as gender) at the beginning.

About the time that the Ask Method was showing me how to rebuild my self-discovery tool, I came across that of a fitness company called Kinobody.[3] Whether you click on "Start here," "Are you a man?" or "Are you a woman?" you get to a page that reads, "Let me show you how to build the body you want—based on where you are right now."

---

3   "Kinobody Fitness," Kinobody, https://kinobody.com/

You move through the brief funnel, selecting your gender (if you haven't already), then general age and condition.

When you complete the questions, the company bets you'll be intrigued enough to find out what it all means. If so, entering your name and email address brings you to a video customized to your answers and an offer of a fitness product that's discounted if you buy now. As a consumer, I bought into the process. As an advertiser, I couldn't wait to adapt it to my business and test it. The questions I used were on the order of "Do you have traffic going to your website?" and "What kind of audience do you have?" The self-discovery tool on our site leads to one in a series of bespoke videos that end in a gentle pitch for our MAP Session—our clients' next level of engagement.

SELF-DISCOVERY TOOLS CAN PRODUCE INSPIRING RESULTS

Seven of the first fifty people who took our self-discovery tool bought our MAP Session at $500, its original price. Based on YouTube's revenue-distribution formula you saw in Chapter 1, we divided our $3,500 by fifty to learn that each person who completed the tool was worth seventy dollars to us. We've since increased the price, naturally.

The self-discovery-tool approach works well for two main reasons:

IT LETS YOU PLAY THE ROLE OF AN EXAMINING DOCTOR INSTEAD OF A PUSHY SALESPERSON

To take the doctor idea to its more literal meaning, let's say you went to a healthcare website to find out whether you had sprained or broken your arm. Assuming that the company's lawyers allowed it, the site might help you decide on your next steps by asking you some doctor-like, exploratory questions: "Where does it hurt? Does it hurt if you do this? How much weight can you lift with that arm?" That's so much more appealing than just "Call this number now and book a session for one hundred dollars."

IT DEMONSTRATES OFFLINE-LIKE EMPATHY

An effective self-discovery tool starts and ends with the customers. It comes from caring about them, considering the kind of interactions they want, and putting yourself in their shoes. It also comes from thinking in an offline way. Although you have access to technological tools, you must never put them ahead of your concern for your audiences.

Let's say that consumers can click on a video of a CEO, not a staff member, giving a clear and useful explanation. That experience might lead viewers to perceive the CEO as a person who cares about them. That feeling is very difficult to recreate in an email.

For my self-discovery tool, I created eight videos tailored

to my prediction of eight potential types of respondents. It was worth the effort to create customized value for each main type of user—to make people feel seen. That's also the thinking behind our choose-your-own-adventure videos...more on that later.

To take the empathy idea further, as a consumer, I fantasize about an online service that would help me choose gifts for my wife. In the fantasy, a department store's website would greet me the same way that a brick-and-mortar shop's representative would: "Do you want help to decide what to buy today?" Yes! For the next two to three minutes, I would answer more questions, such as "Who are you buying for?" and "What types of products does your wife like?"

Based on a glance through my wife's closet and website-supplied product photos, I would know how to answer follow-up questions, such as "What colors does she like? What styles? What labels?" and "What are her sizes?"

At that point, the online personal shopper would give me a list of recommendations along with photos to choose from. I'd click to buy, given the assurance that I could return anything that my wife didn't like. (I can only hope that one reader grabs the idea and runs with it.)

CREATING AN OFFER THAT CONVERTS

When you're considering your product or service offering, make sure you can answer "yes" to each of these questions:

- Will your viewer perceive it as valuable?
- Will your viewer perceive it as desirable?
- Does it logically link to your business and its style?
- Is it easy for the viewer to grasp and accept?
- Is it easy for you to scale (as much as you can handle)?

Once you've created a product or service that rates highly on the four moments of truth and the three factors, you make advertising so much easier and more effective. When people buy, love, and promote your offering, you get a far better return on your ad spend and you can scale your company. In the rest of the book, we'll focus on the search factor, because unless your customers can find you, the other factors are irrelevant.

In the next chapter, you'll learn how to find your customers' moments of need for your product or service, and how to make the most of them.

Mapping Your Customer's Moments: How to Find Those Opportunities

What are your customers going through at their moment of need? What are they searching for? Visualize the whole scenario—from the big picture down to the smallest detail. For example, as soon as I entered my London-Marathon moment, I searched Google and YouTube and read blogs on my cell phone. I was desperate to start buying stuff, morning, noon, and night. Showing you how to identify such moments and visualize the scenario is the goal of this chapter, because when we understand these moments, we can meet them with the right message.

Learning the big picture begins with learning the motivations for your customers' search. When your customers go to YouTube—typically to be inspired (53 percent of visitors, according to Google[1]) or to learn, buy, or do something—they're responding to some "trigger" moment. That trigger can be external (something new coming in) or internal (something coming from within). Map out those trigger moments to begin to analyze how to talk with your customers.

The trigger moment for my decision to run a marathon was external—the WhatsApp message that my friend had pulled out of the running. An example of an internal trigger, on the other hand, would be if I loved running marathons. In that case, my passion would have driven my decision.

The reason to think about the two types of trigger moments is that each is likely to require a different type of message. For example, a physiotherapist who had done that thinking would know better than to try to advertise to every running enthusiast. Doing so would cost much more than sorting out customers by their motivation: people searching for how to run a first marathon need

1   The Consumer Barometer Survey, in response to, "Why did you watch online video(s)" n=2,119, Base: internet users (accessing via computer, tablet or smartphone) who have watched online video in the past week, answering based on a recent online video session, 2014/2015. See Lucas Watson, "Video Micro-Moments: What Do They Mean for Your Video Strategy?" Think with Google, https://www.thinkwithgoogle.com/marketing-resources/micro-moments/video-micro-moments-what-do-they-mean-for-your-video-strategy/

a more basic and informative message than marathon experts who already know they need a physiotherapist and may even have one.

TIMING IS EVERYTHING

Trigger moments are the way to find out how your customers arrived on the path to purchase that we looked at in the previous chapter. They help to determine how to send the right message to the right person at the right time. The framework begins with mapping what sort of moment your customers are having: Is it a window-shopping moment? Is it an in-store moment? Or is it a buying moment?

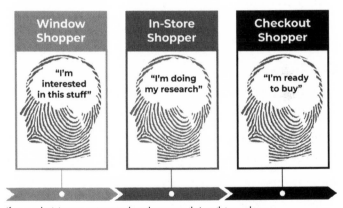

If so, maybe join your customers where they are on their path to purchase.

When I found out my wife and I were pregnant for the second time, I once again became interested in baby-related products. I would have been open to all relevant advertising, so I was a window-shopper for anything in that category. When I needed a double stroller, I became an in-store shopper, going online to see which strollers easily assembled, collapsed, and fit into a car. At that point, I just wanted more information about what I should be looking for and potentially buying. Once I had done my research, I knew what to buy. As a checkout shopper comparing products and watching reviews, the only things I wanted before making my purchase were confidence in my choice and an easy buying experience.

As advertisers, we tend to make online shopping more complicated than it needs to be, and more complicated than customers want it to be. To simplify the process, you need to tailor your messages to those three main types of shopping moments—the positions on the purchase path—and target them using options provided to us by Google AdWords.

Timing can add urgency and connection. To illustrate this point, put yourself in the consumer's place for a moment: If you turned to YouTube because, say, your water heater broke on Christmas Eve, you would be especially grateful to the specialist who created a video that gave you three ways to try to fix it before calling for service. A video like that would engage the persuasion principle of reciprocity because people tend to feel obligated to someone who gives first. Once you had watched the helpful video, if the advice didn't work, that would be the ideal time for the repair company to build on the relationship by offering a deal for service.

Of course, illness also kicks in the urgency factor: Let's say you want to know if you've got a cold or the flu, and whether you need to go to a doctor. A video can tell you how to find out, then send a message: "If you're still not sure, call this number" or "...come to the clinic right away." Give the advertiser extra credit for user experience if the message implies that the doctor or clinic cares about you and not your money.

Another timing consideration is that you might be able to influence customers' position on the path to purchase. In my marathon moment, shoes were my perceived priority, so I moved from being an online shopper to checkout shopper within about thirty seconds. I didn't know to consider a hotel at that time.

But it turned out that hotels on the starting line of the marathon are a hot commodity. A hotel in that location missed the moment to connect with me as early as the day I bought shoes. I would probably have responded to a message such as "If you're thinking about doing the London Marathon and want to stay with us, you should book soon to take advantage of our special VIP Marathon Service. It includes the perfect evening and morning meals and a physiotherapy massage." Of course, when you offer a VIP service, you can charge a lot more.

NEEDS OFTEN OUTRANK WANTS

To me in my marathon moment, a hotel seemed like a "want," while new shoes seemed like a "need." That distinction is still another way of thinking about the trigger moment. Sometimes a moment contains a logical sequence of events. For example, when you plan your wedding, you secure the greatest need first: the venue. Next might come the choice of a photographer or the video team because you need pictures, you know these pros get busy, and you want the best. You wouldn't think about buying flowers, a want—or at least a less-urgent need—before you had sorted out the venue and the pictures.

While I was still focused on running shoes, a physiotherapist was neither a need nor a want, but it became a need soon after I started training. By the point of need, though, my local providers had missed the chance to set themselves apart. Although they had customers who run marathons, they didn't think to map my moments—to target me and others who searched "how to train for a marathon."

All it takes to begin a relationship and lead into the marketing funnel is useful advice (for example, three types of stretches to avoid injury). To get someone to take the next step, including getting on an email database, the physiotherapist could have followed up with a free introductory session. Follow-up promotions or emails with more good advice would have continued that relationship. If, instead, I (the customer) have to wait until the aches and pains show up, the competitive advantage is lost. Everyone's trying to advertise to me at that point.

Not only did I not recognize energy gels as a need or want, I hadn't even *heard* of them until the day before the marathon at the trade exhibition. At the last moment, I was amazed to find out about a product that everyone takes. That was another unmapped moment on the part of the brands. They didn't think to advertise to me before the purchase point. I would've bought any brand I recognized and would've appreciated an early introduction.

I bought on impulse because everyone was buying gels. I ended up choosing, badly, by appearance: I bought red, which I equated with berry flavoring and which seemed more appealing than both the yellow and the fluorescent. The gel turned out to be the worst thing I had ever tasted. I tried it on the starting line, a regrettable marathon launch, but an appropriate symbol of poor user experience.

The mapping gap—missed opportunities—happens all the time in so many industries.

AVOIDING THE MAPPING GAP

The key to avoiding the mapping gap is to think about the customer's journey and where you can tap into it. Think about the points where you have the right and the basis to intersect with that journey and provide a helpful message. When my agency wants to advertise, we focus on what people are typing in when they're promoting their business. We wouldn't use the keywords "YouTube advertising" because not that many people are searching for that phrase yet. Many more people are searching for "how to generate more sales," so we know we can get in front of those searchers with our message about YouTube.

If these people are looking for search engine optimization (SEO) instead, we can send a video message along these lines: "SEO's great, but it's not the most reliable means of generating traffic for your business. You know what is? YouTube advertising." Or maybe they're searching for information about how to run a successful webinar. Surmising that these searchers might want more attendees at their webinar, we would tell them how to boost attendance. Although help with boosting attendance might not be what we sell directly, it's what the user wants, so they'll appreciate the content. Of course, we would also talk about how we use YouTube advertising to fill our own webinars.

Betting against an increase in YouTube traffic would be a huge mistake. According to YouTube, 70 percent of millennials (eighteen- to twenty-four-year-olds) say they can find anything they want to learn on the platform. That 70 percent stat also applies to year-to-year increase of how-to-information searches on YouTube. It's only a matter of time until that attitude expands to their elders. According to an April 2016 Nielsen study, time spent on YouTube from 2015 to 2016 almost tripled among adults age fifty-five and above, growing 80 percent faster than other age ranges.

If you map out your customers' moments—if you know where customers are in their journey, you can show up and be useful, and they'll buy from you. Everyone's crying out for good user experience, yet users typically have to fumble around. If your website visitors do not clearly see what you do in less than three seconds, that's a problem. And if they don't see how to engage with your company in less than ten seconds, that's also a problem. You need to make some changes.

If you instead start off the users' journey correctly, they'll never forget, and you'll have the opportunity to keep them as customers for life.

A TOOL FOR USING YOUTUBE TO UNDERSTAND YOUR CUSTOMERS

"Journey" is also the keyword for a recent experience that reinforces the power of YouTube. For a client whose company promotes health clubs, our agency, Viewability, wanted to discover the moments of its potential customers, so we researched their likely YouTube activity. We began by typing in keywords related to weight loss. The most popular videos we found were about weight-loss journeys: people posting videos to document their transformation from obesity to their ideal weight. These videos get millions of views.

That research revealed a significant customer moment that's unique to YouTube that had escaped us. It also shows that a bit of searching can help you start to identify what your customers might be watching and what they care about. The experience inspired us to create a tool we call the "Title Grabber." Type in a phrase and you'll get the titles of the top 100 videos on that topic. It helps to quickly and clearly identify customer moments. You can find it in the "Book Resources" section on www.viewability.co.uk.

MAPPING MOMENTS WITH EXISTING CUSTOMERS

Every type of moment applies to existing customers, not just to new ones, and Google helps you find these moments. The level of conversation changes, though, as it would in a bricks-and-mortar store. You'll want to create a sense of familiarity, a tailored approach for someone who has engaged with your website before. As a consumer, you've probably experienced "website remarketing": After you look at a product on, say, Amazon, ads for the same product chase you around the web for a few days.

You can do something similar that makes sense, but feels less intrusive, for people who interact with your website. The message might be "Hey, great to see you again. I noticed you watched some videos on the site. Here's something new you might like." While you acknowledge the "familiar faces" of return visitors, you're also reconnecting with them and building a kind of customer-community feel. Be careful not to be creepy, though!

PRACTICAL EXERCISE: FINDING YOUR CUSTOMER MOMENT

Whether you're speaking to existing customers or looking for new ones, it's time for you to turn the theory in this book into practice. Let's choose one moment and map it out. Work on that same moment through the rest of the book to create an ideal ad. (The Title Grabber you just learned about—three paragraphs before this one— will provide insight and inspiration into your customers' thought process.)

Once you've nailed that one moment, come back and create ads for different moments.

Follow this three-step process:

1. Start by thinking about your customer and mapping the whole path of moments before they come to you.

For example, let's say you're that rare physiotherapist who targets people who search "how to run a marathon." That's one of many possible moments. As you reflect on your customers, you may start to identify that a lot of your regulars are senior citizens who put their back out when they garden every spring. You let that fact inspire your choice of moment, and it's not when they search for the keywords "back pain." A more exclusive moment to advertise to them might be when they begin looking for gardening ideas.

As a second example, let's say we're mapping customer moments for a business coach. Their customers might be looking up "how to grow my business," "how to become a speaker," "how to get published," or "how to attract a new category of clients."

2. Choose one moment: Imagine you're painting a picture of the moment or taking a snapshot of it in your mind.

Determine what that moment looks like. Fill in the demographic and other defining details such as age, location, household income, parental status, the kind of device, and the time of day. Then paint the whole scenario. Later, we might create twenty ads for each moment that individual people experience. But in this moment, for this person, we're painting this picture:

> This customer is a thirty-five-year-old female entrepreneur who has struggled in her business for four years. She thinks the best thing she could do right now is attract high-level speaking engagements and media spots to position herself as an expert. She's searching on her desktop in the middle of the day, and her office looks like this...

You can tap into the emotion behind that sense of "struggle" to write a powerful ad for that person. It's as if you're writing an ad for your best friend; your caring will come across as authentic.

The more details you can fill in, the more authentically you can speak to your customer. Perhaps surprisingly, that authenticity comes through even when you've had to make up some of the details. It's the sharpening of the picture in your mind that leads to a connected message.

3. Use that picture to create the ideal scenario for the customer.

At this point in your crawl inside your customer's head, you should start to feel as though you can say something worthwhile in that moment to that customer.

This part bears repeating because it's key: Make sure you're talking to one person at this particular moment, not a number and not a crowd. Don't focus on reach and frequency. The fact that at least thousands of people might be having the same moment every day is beside the point. You're basically saying, "I can write a good ad for this one person because I connect with her, and I know exactly what she's thinking and going through."

Talking to one person makes the process so much easier, less intimidating, and more successful because you're not straining to write brilliant copy to get thousands of people to buy. You just need to get that one person to buy—many, many times over. It's as if that person is many different "one persons." Because you're targeting a moment a lot of people experience, you can speak in a way that resonates with them as individuals.

Maybe you've had the same powerful consumer experience with an online ad that so speaks to your needs that it almost seems to read your mind. That's exactly what you need to achieve for your customer.

WHAT GOOGLE *CAN'T* DO FOR YOU

It's unlikely that Google's artificial intelligence will be up to creating and presenting the ideal message to convert viewers into customers anytime soon, so those tasks are up to you. In the following chapter, you'll learn about how to go about crafting the most appropriate message for your customer's moment.

The Message for the Moment: How to Define It

Now that you've thought about your customers, mapped their moments, and chosen one of those moments, you realize how much easier it is to speak to a person in that scenario. If you were to meet that person in real life, you might already know what to say and how to say it.

You would know to use a tone of voice and communication style that, rather than going into TV-presenter mode, is like speaking one-on-one. Although millions of people may be seeing your video, you would be able to visualize being helpful in a chat to that one person who's watching the video on a phone, iPad, or computer. You would be able to visualize not being sleazy.

As I write this, I'm just an hour past witnessing "sleazy." While picking up my car from service at the dealership, I overheard a pushy pitch by a salesman on autopilot: "Here's what's great about this car, why you should get it, and what the financing is." The salesman never bothered to ask his "target," the shopper, what she needed and wanted.

A lot of the promotions found online suffer from the same affliction. What guards against that affliction is caring about the customer's moment, because doing so helps you switch to a consultative *listening* mode. It helps you respond to what you've learned the customer is going through.

EVOLVE TO INVOLVE

Meeting the moment and finding what works starts with the right state of mind, which Benjamin Franklin reputedly found appropriate words to describe long before video existed: "Tell me and I forget. Teach me and I remember. Involve me and I learn." When my agency started out, our thirty-second videos looked and sounded like TV ads that "tell me and I forget." They talked at the customer—"I've got this amazing thing. Sign up here." It worked, but it was by no means the best we could have done.

YouTube provided the justification for the tell-me

approach, and it continues to do so: The ad was free when someone clicked to the website or away within thirty seconds, so we rushed to grab the free clicks under the wire. But the problem with just grabbing clicks was that people weren't remembering the videos or the business.

We turned our attention to the next line in the saying: "Teach me and I remember."

USE THE ADUCATE FORMULA

When we began standardizing on the idea of content first, we realized we were going past pure promotion and using education as the core of the message. Our agency coined the term "ADUCATE" and turned it into an acronym that represents the seven points of an effective business script.

A: Aim
D: Difficulty
U: Understanding
C: Credibility
A: Action Plan
T: Teach
E: Exit

Inspired by the famous print campaigns of David Ogilvy, the godfather of advertising, we invented this ADUCATE system so we could get scripts right every time. We find it particularly useful for getting started, especially when we're not feeling at our creative best. This structure, which we used data to refine, has served us well in creating video ads for products and services, and it will serve you well, too.

A is for **Aim—your viewer's aim.** This video you're creating needs to bring the viewer (or audience, if you prefer) what they want. What do they want in particular, and what will it mean to them to get it in general? Love? Health? Success? Tap into their innermost desires, whatever you're promoting. So, who is your customer, and what is their aim? What do they really want? Within the first five seconds, the viewer needs to know this video ad is relevant to their needs and desires.

D is for **Difficulty.** Most people go to YouTube because they want information that can help them achieve their aim, but something stands in their way. They can't achieve it because maybe what they want to do is too complicated and they need someone to simplify it for them. Or maybe they just can't find the information they seek. For every business, there's always some level of difficulty.

Let's say the viewer wants improved health, but conflicting advice confuses them. If you're the advertiser, then, and you acknowledge that difficulty, you can mirror the conversation going on in the viewer's mind. In doing so, you start to build trust with them. Give yourself bonus points if you can personify that difficulty.

Some TV ads for kitchen cleansers do a great job of personifying difficulty, and they need to. Just saying that the product kills bacteria wouldn't inspire anyone. But turn that bacteria into a green monster that you can dissolve with the spray and you get a different reaction. Allstate Insurance also found an effective way to personify difficulty: a human character named Mayhem who destroys homes and cars.

U is for **Understanding**. Show you understand your audience's emotions, not just their situation, and that you get how they feel. If you can effectively convey that empathy, even in a few sentences, you will bond with them.

C is for **Credibility**. Position yourself as an expert in your viewer's eyes with a quick statement about how many people you've helped out of the same difficulty. You can also demonstrate credibility by mentioning books you've written or showing footage of presentations you've given; business awards you've won; or five-star reviews, testimonials, or celebrity endorsements your products have received. You need no more than one or two sentences for this because you've already won over the viewer by demonstrating your empathetic understanding.

A is for **Action Plan**. Expressing one can build even more trust in you because it shows that you not only understand the difficulty, but you also know what to do about it. Even if your customer has twenty-seven things to do, I recommend condensing them into a manageable-sounding plan with only three or four steps.

You get bonus points if the plan includes a first step that the customer has already completed, so they've got momentum going for them. I recently wrote an educational script about software that helps people create websites. The three steps are to choose your niche as a business, think about your branding, and build your website. Most people who watch the video will feel as though they've mastered the first step.

Many coffee shops that offer loyalty programs have also learned that shortcuts pay off. Loyalty cards that require customers to receive ten stamps for a free coffee and that give them two stamps on their first visit are far more powerful than cards that require only eight stamps but give customers none on their first visit. The psychological technique works because it helps people feel that they've already begun the journey to success.

T is for **Teach**. Bring your action plan to life for your viewer by giving them some context and teaching them something. The *teaching* section of the video is a powerful way to show the viewer how they will use the action plan. If you are able to show the viewer a unique feature or a brand-new tip, they will not only get a glimpse of the value your product or service can provide, they will also begin to imagine themselves using your action plan to finally achieve their aims. You'll get extra bonus points here if you are able to wrap up this teaching section in a real-world case study, as this will give the viewer a story to remember. At the end of the teaching section, we really want the viewer to be thinking, "That's amazing; how do I find out more?"

When you've delivered the context, it's time for the bridge between the teaching section and the ending. Build in more credibility and trust with "The Power of the But," a persuasive technique I learned from psychologist and author Robert Cialdini. Start by highlighting some genuine, small drawback of the product or service. Audiences tend to see your openness about the imperfection as proof of trustworthiness. The pre-"but" statement can even be humorous, as in this example: "Product X probably won't help your kids sleep through the night, but it will do this: (fill in the blank with what viewers want to achieve)."

Then use the tiny conjunction "but" to deliver the strongest element of your offering. The technique adds emotional context, dilutes what you said before, and calls attention to what follows. An auto manufacturer once broke the rule with a statement to shareholders like this:

"The financial review looks good, but it will take a long time to implement." Simply flipping the statement to "It will take a long time to implement, but the financial review looks good" makes it so much more persuasive.

For example, "Our restaurant is small, but that's what makes the atmosphere cozy" turns what some people might view as a flaw into a strength. The line also meets this second requirement: What follows the "but" must relate to what came before it because the word triggers the brain to pay close attention. Note the difference in this line, which lacks a logical relationship: "Our restaurant is small, but we have a big parking lot."

The persuasive value of the word "but" is rooted in typical childhood experiences. As a child, you quickly learned to associate the word with negative connotations. One of your parents or a teacher probably told you that you were doing something well. Then you heard the "but" that introduced criticism and ruined the moment, causing you to forget everything you heard before the word.

E is for **Exit**. Leave the viewer with a clear restatement of your product or service, what they'll gain if they take action, and what they'll lose if they don't. People who feel as though they're losing something tend to want it more. Be subtle about the loss part, though, because you want to remain on friendly terms with the viewer. Take the role of a trusted advisor to suggest that not taking action leaves them with the same problem.

You'll earn more bonus points and more business if you can tie that gain into how viewers perceive themselves. Gently suggest that the choice they make at this moment—to click or not—reflects who they are as a person. For someone who wants to learn to advertise more effectively, you might say something like this: "The people who get great results and can call themselves ad pros know that taking action is the first step."

Finally, "future pace" the choice. Walk the viewer through what to expect once they click the button to the website. You'll bump up conversion rates—the number of people who take some action on your page—by showing what the website looks like and exactly how to fill out the form to get access to the offer.

HOW THE BRAIN *REALLY* WORKS AND ENGAGES

Let's look more deeply at the brain (than we did in the Introduction) to see why engagement matters and how memories stick. Cognitive psychologist David Rubin's exercise illustrates the brain's interconnectedness. Memories, he found, don't exist in isolation. This information superseded the outdated theory that the brain is like a file cabinet that stores memories in folders.

Rubin found that the act of simply asking people to recall a popular song would trigger a whole memory structure. The structure might begin with the experience of almost hearing the song, sung by the artist. The memory then might become more vivid and involved; people typically recall things such as the first or last time they heard the song and with whom.

The exercise engages people's senses with other cues, including asking participants to recall the taste of a watermelon. Instead of directly summoning taste, though, many people think of the fruit's look and texture first.

One of the more challenging requests of the exercise is to recall the definition of "truth." Most people try to picture it in the dictionary or think of their parents teaching them about the concept.

Rubin, who compared the brain to Velcro's loops and memories to its hooks, concluded that we tend to remember *everything* about a memorable experience, but with some parts clearer than others. The longer, more frequent, or more intense the experience, the more hooks it creates to connect memories to the brain's loops.

The ability of that song, that taste, and that concept to spark emotions and related memories mirrors the ability of video to do the same. When you provide a good video experience, it's as if you've attached yourself to people's brains. It would be difficult to detach, even if you *wanted* to. That fact means that, along with sticking to people's brains, you need to make sure you're sticking appropriately. If you create videos people enjoy and find useful, they'll remember you for all the right reasons.

Give yourself extra credit if your videos can naturally evoke touch (or a feeling), taste, and smell, not only sight and sound. But even if they can't do so, now you know that viewers' brains are capable of making those sensory connections for themselves.

A close friend of mine, Alex Hormozi, recently gave me some incredible insight for a client I work with in the weight loss industry.

He suggested that in the video my client should ask viewers to take part in an exercise where they were instructed to grab their stomach and hold as much belly fat in their hands as possible. Then ask the viewer to focus on the amount they were holding in their hands and what they are going to do about it.

Needless to say, this dramatically improved the campaign performance. Thanks Alex!

Viewers are more likely to make those connections when you've customized videos to fit the moments along that path to purchase you learned about in Chapter 1.

Whenever you create a YouTube ad, use a single core

message to stick to mental loops. As soon as you try to deliver more than one message in a video, people forget it. Choose your core message and delete any part of your video that does not support it.

If finding a single core message is difficult for you, remember to put yourself in your customer's moments and shoes, as the previous chapters suggested. What can also help you to both choose a message and set the video's tone is to assess yourself, with the help of these questions:

- What do you stand for?
- What do you stand against?

As proof of the value of the questions, especially the second one, let's take the example of an internet radio station I heard about years ago. Its first slogan—"We play rock 24/7"—expressed what the station stood for, and it worked well enough. But almost as soon as the station changed its slogan to what it stood against—"You'll never hear Justin Bieber or Lady Gaga here"—it multiplied its listener base.

The method also works because standing against something tends to harness more energy and passion than standing for it. That passion can become easier for an audience to identify with.

SCHEMA VIOLATIONS: THE *WHAT THE HELL?* APPROACH TO GETTING ATTENTION

Of course, to be able to share compelling content, the audience must be willing to let you. The best way to turn window-shoppers—the toughest audience to crack—into attentive video viewers is to open with something unexpected yet related to the core message.

Psychology provides a term for the unexpected: "schema violation." A schema is our mental model of the world. A violation of that schema works because we humans are wired to notice and respond to differences in our environment. This behavior is a key survival mechanism. We've evolved to react that way even when our survival doesn't depend on it.

We've also evolved to create patterns for almost everything we do on a regular basis, such as engaging in a morning routine. Those patterns include the details—not just *that* and *when* you brush your teeth, but also which hand you use to hold the brush and how you apply the toothpaste. You quickly turn the process into a routine because it saves time and energy. Once you learn it or once you form a perception of what things look like, you don't have to think about it.

Anything new thrown into that pattern, then, gets our attention. A recent example of a schema violation occurred on my first day in my agency's new location. I didn't know that entry requires a key card, so I couldn't figure out how to get in until the laughing receptionist came to my aid.

I know how to open doors, but this system's design didn't fit into all I had learned and always practiced, so it caught my full attention. The embarrassment of having people witness my failure added an emotional element to make the experience all the more compelling. To shake off that uncomfortable feeling, I rushed into learning mode. At that point, if someone had told me that, to open the door, I would have to tap my knees three times and scratch my left ear, I probably would've tried it.

That's the beauty of a video that begins with a schema violation related to the core message: It opens the viewer's mind and lets you insert your message and make it stick. As an example, Frank Kern, one of our clients, began a video by talking about how he was thrown out of a strip joint on a Monday afternoon, "but," he said, "it's not what you think." After such a strange opener, viewers almost *have* to keep watching. Then came the kicker, the relationship to the message: "At that moment, I swore I would never go cold-call selling again."

Kern went on to talk about the more effective type of selling that he was about to teach in the video. Then he taught it and wrapped up, appropriately, with the call to action.

We also tested the attention-getting opener for Amy Porterfield, who teaches people how to market their businesses. She started by saying how much she hates consulting. For window-shoppers, that opener did better than one without an attention-getter.

For in-store customers in research mode who are typing in keywords, though, that same video garnered the opposite results: Going directly into the advice worked better than starting with an attention-getter—more proof that you need a different message for a difference audience.

It's not easy to think of a great schema violation, though, so you could start by experimenting with one of these approaches:

- Direct a question to the viewer, using the word "you." A question tends to work because the viewer isn't expecting one. What's more, our brains find it difficult *not* to engage with a question. The "Did you know...?" format has tested particularly well.
- Set the stage for a mystery. Pose the topic, then say something like, "We *thought* (fill-in-the-blank idea), but we were wrong, and here's why... Next we tried (fill-in-the-blank action), which worked better, but it

still wasn't right. Here's why." You might add one or two more tried-and-abandoned items before finally giving the punch line. The approach works because viewers *want* to solve the mystery, so they carefully listen for clues.

OTHER TIPS TO INCREASE ENGAGEMENT

Shoot the boss: We tend to standardize on a human presenter, which enables valuable human connection. When that presenter is also the brand's founder, it enhances the potential to add credibility, authority, and personality to the brand.

Tailor the format: Gear the content to the message. In most cases, a product begs for a demonstration, and this is perfect to include in the teaching section of your video ad. The message also might need some simple slides with applicable graphics or just a few words on each display.

Offer the tip of the iceberg: Make clear that those three or so tips you're giving away are certainly useful, yet only a small slice of the value you can offer. The viewer tends to feel a sense of completion while being drawn toward taking the next step to the bigger prize. Remember, you want viewers to think, "Thank you; that was awesome. What's next?"

Say the phrase and words that pay: Almost as important

as finding the right content is using persuasive words to deliver it. For example, after you've said what you'll share in the rest of the video, explain what it means for the viewer, starting with three powerful little words: "**So you can**," which links the hook to its benefit and helps you remember to focus on the viewer.

For example, "I'll show you three things to look for when you shop for a double stroller, *so you can* find the right one for yourself and avoid expensive mistakes." Or, "I'll share how to find your prospects, *so you can* get more leads and make more sales."

In ADUCATE, earlier in this chapter, you learned The Power of the But. Another powerful b-word, "**because**," suggests that something is important. University researchers proved the value of "because" in experiments with people lining up for a photocopier. The researchers asked whether they could cut in. Some people allowed it; some didn't. But when researchers gave a reason—"because I've got to get this report in" or "because I'm really late"—more people in line agreed.

Unlike "but" follow-ups, what comes after "because" doesn't need a strong relationship with what precedes it (although a strong relationship doesn't *hurt*). People tend to feel more confident if they hear any reason at all. The photocopier experiments yielded the same results even when researchers tried random strings of excuses after "because." Something ridiculous, such as "because I like oranges," would have worked, too. The word itself adds the perception of value to what comes before.

Along with knowing which words to use, also consider the impact of the occasional and brief **absence of words**. Long pauses can emphasize what's before and after them; they can also give viewers space to consider and absorb the message. Appropriate and well-placed music can tug on emotions.

As our agency has proven again and again—ADUCATE viewers and they'll remember the brand. Now let's take Ben Franklin's advice and go one step further than teaching viewers. Let's involve them.

ADUCATE MEETS CHOICE—CHOOSE YOUR OWN ADVENTURE

At Viewability, we've begun testing a new way of working with ADUCATE: letting viewers tailor the information for themselves. This powerful new technique deserves a section of its own because it so effectively inspires engagement. We've found that creating a good customer experience often means creating different experiences for different types of customers. To find out what type of customer you're addressing in your video, ask the customers themselves to tell you where they belong.

I was inspired to apply this technique to videos after I rediscovered the Choose Your Own Adventure books my brother and I had read as kids. After a paragraph or so, those books would give the reader an option, such as "If you want to have this adventure, turn to page 6. If you want to explore that adventure, turn to page 38." More forks in the road would follow each choice, which made the experience almost like reading a new story each time.

Call it serendipity: My brainstorm arrived at the same time YouTube introduced "end screens"—clickable links in videos that work on all devices. This feature improves viewers' ability to click from one video to up to four.

Here's one example of the method in action: Tony Pole-castro, a client who gives guitar lessons, tends to attract two types of audiences (beginners and experienced players who are in a rut). So, after saying he'll offer valuable information in the video, he segments his viewers by letting them group themselves and put themselves in charge: "To tailor this information to you from here on in, I need to know where you are with the guitar. If you're a beginner, click the 'New to Guitar?' button right now. If you're a player who's in a rut, click 'In a Guitar Rut?'"

If you are wondering how we are able to insert the clickable "New to Guitar?" and "In a Guitar Rut?" video links, we use a feature called "end screens" that you will be able to find inside of your YouTube account in the video's "Info & Settings" section.

Each group benefits from customized information without having to leave a name or an email address. The commitment is minimal, yet sufficient to invoke another of Cialdini's persuasive principles, "Commitment and Consistency." Once you start a journey, you're unlikely to stop it halfway. The viewer is likely to take the next step, or click, in this case, and then sign up for the workshop Tony promotes.

Meanwhile, Tony has learned more about his audience, and he's enjoying brilliant results, again proving the financial value of great user experience. He has earned 33 percent more registrations for his workshop, 52 percent more sales, and a 39 percent increase in view rate. (Google relies on its view-rate metric—how long people watch—to grant more exposure.)

Perhaps most valuable is that Tony has also received this intelligence about his audience: Of all the viewers, those who self-identified as being in a rut bought five times more often than those that chose the "new" option. That tells us where to focus future efforts.

By the way, those calls to action are almost immediate. None of these videos ask viewers to come to a website before they can begin their adventure. Instead, the message is "Let's start the adventure now," on YouTube.

SIMPLIFY AND TEST—DON'T PERFECT

As you plan your first video ad, it's important to remember that you should not even think about trying to make a masterpiece or spending a lot of time or money. For most industries and audiences, good information is much more important than TV-quality production values. Keep your videos simple, especially your first ones. You've got to get started to know how to do better the next time.

"Simple" means shooting in a studio and creating the video for less than $1,000, in most cases. Consider spending more only if you're selling a luxury brand. (If $1,000 seems too high, you might weigh that cost against your potential ROI. Then compare it to the least you would have to spend for TV advertising's inferior returns.)

DELEGATE PROFESSIONAL PRODUCTION

Although you shouldn't concern yourself with perfection, also don't let poor production values drive away viewers. At the very least, your video needs to look professional. Rather than consider what camera to buy or how to shoot or edit the video, plan to delegate those tasks to an expert. We do; even with all the videos our agency creates, and even though we're building a studio in-house for training and blog videos, we'll continue to go outside to a professional studio for our clients' work.

Commissioning a local videographer or studio isn't that expensive. A studio will cost around $500 a day, plus a videographer (if needed), equipment, and a video editor. It's worth budgeting for a good editor who can turn your raw footage into something amazing. If your budget requires the lowest end, though, you could seek out a university student with a portfolio of professional videos.

DON'T DELEGATE THE SCRIPT

With the ADUCATE and choose-your-own-adventure principles, combined with your knowledge of your customers and their moments, you're more qualified to write the script for your YouTube videos than any copywriter you could commission. Contractors might be able to write a good script for TV or Facebook, but it won't work for what's unique about YouTube and how viewers interact with the platform.

You can't expect a script written for those other platforms to be successful on YouTube. For one thing, people are more likely to watch a YouTube video, where they might scroll past a video on Facebook. For another, YouTube viewers also tend to watch videos with the sound on, as opposed to those on Facebook. What's more, a repurposed ad for one platform also won't incorporate the other techniques you're learning about in this book.

PUTTING IT ALL TOGETHER

In this chapter, you've learned about ADUCATE and other successful scripting and formatting techniques. Now let's turn those building blocks into the nuts and bolts of building a video campaign to reach your customers. That's coming up next.

Meeting the Moment: The Logistics of Making It Happen

You've chosen that one moment, you've written the script, and you've got your video. Everything you've learned so far will stand the test of time. This chapter guides you through the next step: how to get your video in front of your users.

As you would probably guess, the first thing to do is to sign up for a YouTube account. Inside of that account, you'll create your channel, which houses your videos. You can brand the channel, and the platform provides simple tutorials with guidelines for customizing the channel.

Design, though, like production and post-production, is important enough to get right, so consider delegating that, too. But if you insist on doing it yourself and you don't have a design background, you can find some decent templates on websites such as canva.com.

Now move to the AdWords website and follow the instructions to open an account there, too. Get help, if you need it, from free tutorials on that site, on YouTube, or on www.viewability.co.uk. To fund the account, it probably makes sense to start small. Even limiting the budget to ten dollars a day—and limiting the maximum cost per view—can earn you a lot of traffic. Also, what you learn in your early video campaigns will guide you as you scale.

Of course, Google tracks what websites you visit, when you visit them, what you do there, and how long you stay. Although that can feel a little creepy, you can console yourself by remembering the ways in which that intelligence benefits you: As a consumer, advertisers have the potential to help you with the moments of need in your life. More to the point of this book, as an advertiser, you learn enough about your potential customers to find, attract, and help them. We can do so if we know how to use this information, and that's where AdWords comes in.

A POWERFUL MIX: SEARCH, VIDEO, AND ADWORDS

As you visualize and prepare to execute your video, it's a great time to review the basics: why people search and how YouTube and AdWords support the experience, bringing together searchers and advertisers in greater numbers every day.

- **Search**: People are searching YouTube for four main reasons: to learn, do, or buy something, or to be inspired.

- **Video**: Even though people also search other platforms, some searches lend themselves to YouTube because video optimizes the experience for the viewer. Searchers soon begin interacting with videos, which can create strong engagement.

- **AdWords**: You're using the power of AdWords to connect your perfect video with your perfect customer. The various targeting options of AdWords link to those four reasons people are searching.

To get a more vivid picture of how the combination works, let's return to the example of my stroller **search**. As soon as my wife and I began searching for what we would need for our second child, some advertiser could have easily anticipated those needs with a **video**. If they had shown me a demonstration of the stroller's use (for example, dismantling, loading into the car, and reassembling), it's very likely that I would have bought their product.

Keywords on **AdWords** give clues to a searcher's position on the path to purchase. My search entry, "best stroller 2014," indicated that I was probably at the beginning of my buying cycle. If instead I had searched for a specific brand name or a comparison of a few named brands, the advertiser could surmise that I was about to buy and could tailor the message accordingly.

Be creative with keywords. In the case of a stroller search, advertisers of other products would have done well to heed the hint of a family's imminent expansion. It would be a great time to offer, say, details or a test-drive of "the safest (bigger) family cars on the road."

SOME ADWORDS TARGETING OPTIONS

At least that's where AdWords *should* come in. Advertisers often know that targeting options exist with Google and Facebook, but until you read this book, you might not realize these options are also available with YouTube ads.

One option you and your audience members will appreciate is the ability to limit the number of times—maybe to once a day—any user can see your ad. That's because there's a fine line between being responsive and being a nuisance. Avoiding bombarding people with the same ad also has the advantage of limiting your cost.

You can also choose between the following two types of video ads. Both allow you to get free exposure for your brand and to pay only for clicks or for viewers you engage. These two types of ads form YouTube's TrueView advertising—where you only pay for a "true" view or engagement.

IN-STREAM

Also known as "pre-roll," in-stream ads pop up before the video the consumer planned to watch. This is the type most people know because they also know where to pounce on the "Skip Ad" button to get to the video they chose. That's why you need a pattern interrupt or strong hook in those first five seconds before the exit hatch appears.

With in-stream ads, you pay only when a viewer clicks to your website or watches thirty seconds or the whole of your video. Even in those cases, you don't have to pay much if you control your maximum cost per view.

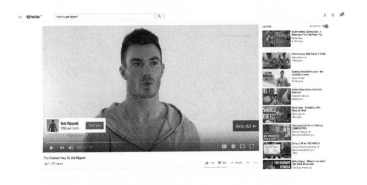

DISCOVERY

Formerly called "in-display" or "in-search," these ads are the one or two that show up above the "organic" (high-ranking, most relevant) videos on the search-results page. In this case, you pay only when someone clicks to play your video. Compared with in-stream ads, discovery ads typically get fewer clicks and views, which means less engagement. They can still be useful, though, because they're so visible. In addition to appearing on the search-results page, they also can turn up as a suggested video to the right of a video someone chose to watch. This page is called the watch page. You can also choose to appear on YouTube's home page when you run discovery ads.

You pay only at the beginning of the video if someone decides to click and play it. In the case of discovery ads, you get free brand exposure when searchers see the thumbnail all over YouTube.

BUMPER ADS

A relatively new YouTube offering, the bumper ad is becoming popular, especially in our agency, because it can work very well. It's a six-second video ad that is designed to tease the viewer and raise brand awareness. It's a great way to prime your audience—you can show a longer ADUCATE-style video to all those people that first saw the bumper ad. It's almost like a trailer for the main video.

For example, we recently shot some bumper ads of the presenter seemingly behind the scenes (with the studio in the background) and between shoots. In the first five seconds, the presenter mentioned that they were shooting some new videos that were going to be really helpful for "you." Then in the final second, to further prime the audience, we edited in some animation saying, "NEW VIDEO COMING SOON."

Although we'll need more testing before we can say we have mastered the approach, the early results for these types of campaigns have showed great promise. View rates have increased dramatically—viewers who are primed watch far more of the ADUCATE video. Conversions have had their own dramatic increase.

While the user experience (UX) is also improved, getting the campaign, including bumper ads, to be a financial success requires concentration and extra effort. Unlike in-stream and discovery ads, for which you pay per view, bumper ads rack up costs per 1,000 impressions (CPM). Also, when you calculate the conversion cost for this type of approach, remember to add the cost of following up with other ads.

HARNESSING THE INTELLIGENCE OF GOOGLE AND ADWORDS

For all three types of ads, though, your chances of getting in front of the right person at the right time are very high, because Google, AdWords, and their algorithms are on the case. They help you target by age, gender, parental status, and any or all of the other demographics the platforms track.

Another demographic option lets you advertise—in the US and in Canada, so far—to people in the top 10 percent, 20 percent, 30 percent, 40 percent, 50 percent, or lower 50 percent of household income—or to any other bracket. You can target by location down to specific ZIP codes, and you can choose "radius targeting," where you select your ads' geographic reach (for example, twenty-three miles around the center of Boston). You can also target by time of day or by type of device: mobile versus tablet versus computer, for example.

Or, you might find you learn more at first by keeping your options open.

But we've only just scratched the surface. Let's look at the various targeting options that Google provides and what they can do for us.

VIDEO-PLACEMENT TARGETING

Video placements are individual videos on YouTube. They enable you to run your in-stream ads in front of any video you choose (as long as the content creator of that video placement has allowed advertising on that video, which is often the case).

When you've identified your customer's moment, you can choose video placements—videos that are relevant for that moment. By doing so, you'll likely get good results because you're literally interrupting potential customers at exactly the right time with the right video ad.

If you're new to YouTube advertising, start with placements because they provide granular data on the performance of each video where viewers find your ad. Google data on how placement performed for you will tell you whether to spend more, spend less, or stop advertising on any particular placement.

Google and AdWords offer further help: You can type in keywords to get a list of links to relevant video placements. The process of working with these links used to take a lot of time until our agency developed software applications that work with YouTube and let you collect many placements for each keyword you might search. So, you can simply copy and paste all the relevant links into your ad campaign and get going. In fact, we have provided free versions of our different software applications in the "book resources" section of www.viewability.co.uk.

We typically use this type of targeting for the videos that in-store shoppers are likely to watch when they are looking to learn, do, or buy something.

CHANNEL-PLACEMENT TARGETING

Similar to video-placement targeting, which lets you choose videos, channel-placement targeting lets you choose an entire channel and all the videos within it.

For example, let's say I'm selling a new type of baby bottle designed to help babies with acid reflux. I *could* grab all the relevant videos related to "best baby bottles" or "how to stop acid reflux." But you could choose all baby-related channels and advertise across all the videos within them. Google helps you find those channels, not just videos, and keep a close eye on your numbers.

TOPIC TARGETING

AdWords also categorizes YouTube videos by topic and subtopic. Returning to the baby-bottle scenario, we could test a variety of topics easily found in your AdWords account. For example, they might include "Nursery & Playroom," "Baby & Pet Names," "Parenting," "Babies & Toddlers," "Baby & Toddler Toys," "Baby Care & Hygiene," "Baby Food & Formula," and "Pregnancy & Maternity."

When you target topics, you're more likely to get in front of in-store shoppers—when they look for videos that are relevant to that topic. Topic is a slightly broader targeting category than placements. That means that, although it might enable faster scaling, topic targeting won't give you as much granular control.

KEYWORD TARGETING

This targeting option is my favorite way to find in-store shoppers. It gives you the ability to advertise to people looking for relevant content, as other targeting methods do, but with the addition of a huge ability to scale. When choosing keyword targeting, your ads will show to users based on their recent browsing history. Google research suggests "recent" might mean forty minutes, but the window of time matters less than the results. This means that if the user were to type a keyword into YouTube or Google, and then watch videos on YouTube, your ads could show to that user.

To take advantage of the scaling opportunity that this targeting option provides, be as specific as possible when you choose keywords. For example, instead of "public speaking," you would probably need to narrow the focus to something like "how to give a business presentation."

Top Tip: Sometimes a keyword shows a lot of promise in terms of scale, but it's a little too expensive for you to justify using it as a targeting option, even after you play with the cost per view, create better videos, or isolate the best-performing demographic data. In those instances, it might be worth adding a relevant topic to layer onto the keyword campaign. We call this (appropriately enough) a "Keyword Plus Topic" campaign. You still get to advertise to users who have recently searched your keyword, but only while they're still looking at relevant videos. This layered targeting means you're targeting people when they are in their exact moment of need and the cost of acquiring that viewer as a lead or customer is likely to be a lot lower.

WEBSITE REMARKETING

When users watch your video ad and click to your website, you know they are interested in what you have to offer. They also now know who you are, so they have moved much closer to becoming a checkout shopper. But, of course, not every website visitor will turn into a customer right away—some will leave your website before buying anything or registering their details to grab your free offer. (I know, the nerve of them!)

If you install a remarketing pixel (a section of code you can find inside your AdWords account's "Shared Library") on your website, you'll be able to "tag" your visitors based on the pages they visit. The tags will enable you to add these visitors to a list of remarketing audiences you create, for up to 540 days. But start with one-day, three-day, seven-day, and thirty-day lists. Then you can choose to target these audiences with more video ads.

Additionally, you can get back in front of people that visit your website from other sources: If people initially visited your website from a promotion you're running on Facebook, you can also target those people on YouTube.

If you decide to exclude all visitors who bought or registered, website remarketing lets you target checkout shoppers who did not buy or register the first time around. But those customers know you and did not take action on your website for a reason, so carefully consider the message and offer you use as a follow-up; what might work for this audience is a familiar message but a different offer. Remarketing requires practicing restraint so you don't annoy people or, worse, seem like a stalker!

Some charities have demonstrated an appropriate balance. For example, donors to a yearly event might receive a "thank you" message along with what's known as a "conversion pixel" to tag them. Later in the year, you can target all those people that donated to encourage another donation. More effective than just a request and a call to action, though, would be a message like this: "Thank you so much for your recent donation. Here's what your contribution achieved..."

In that case, leave out the call to action; not every communication needs to be a pitch. Instead, model your behavior on how people want you to treat them in the real world—as people, not numbers or dollar signs.

In fact, when it's helpful, customers actually *appreciate* remarketing. I'm thinking about my typical experience when I'm in the market for air travel. I might take a couple of days to buy the flight. First, I might window-shop or consult a calendar or the client I'm planning to meet. Then, I move on to other tasks. When I'm ready to return to the task, relevant remarketing ads speed me back to the last point in my decision process; I don't have to start from scratch. Other searchers who tend to appreciate remarketing are those who simply get distracted, which applies to most people at various times.

VIDEO REMARKETING

Another possibly welcome application of remarketing is to run new ads to people who've watched your videos. Set up that ability in the AdWords "Shared Library." Inside "Audiences," choose "YouTube users" to get a choice of remarketing lists based on people's interactions with your videos. For example, you might target ads to those who subscribe to your channel, who watched a particular video, or especially who liked or commented on a video. Then you'll know to offer people more of what they've shown they like.

GOOGLE CUSTOMER MATCH

This feature is a great way of promoting a new product or

service to your existing database. It lets you upload a data file of the email addresses of your leads or customers. You can then create campaigns to target these customers and they will see your ads as they visit YouTube.

You can also use the feature to ensure that customers who recently bought your product are happy with their purchase. Target them with helpful ads about how to use your product.

SIMILAR AUDIENCES

When you upload your email list, AdWords automatically builds a "similar audience" list—typically ten times the size of the list you upload. But although these people are similar to those on your customer or prospect list, they are unlikely to know you or your business, so they are most like window-shoppers.

Google also automatically generates a list of similar audiences from your website and conversion data. It tracks any new registrants or buyers who reach "thank you" pages in which a pixel is installed; these audiences can be huge—much bigger than ten times the size of the similar-audience list built from your email list. So, the more you advertise, the better and bigger similar audiences can become!

AFFINITY-AUDIENCE TARGETING

These audiences, which come predefined from Google, are great for reaching—at scale—potential customers who have shown a strong interest in a specific subject. For instance, if you are a keen photographer, you'll likely be visiting various photography websites and reviewing photography-related products. Google will be tracking your behavior and, as such, they will add you to their "shutterbugs" affinity audience category. As an advertiser, if I had a business selling cameras and photography accessories, it might be worth running a test campaign to target "shutterbugs," as they are likely to be interested in what I had to offer.

Now, because these audiences have been built for companies that want to cost-effectively extend the reach of TV campaigns onto the web, this targeting option is typically used for brand awareness, not ROI. So although you may find some huge audiences that seem like a good fit for your products, I would tread very carefully if you want to get a strong ROI. By all means, test these audiences, as they can work, but I would recommend layering the targeting with keyword or topic targeting to drive a better ROI.

Learning to work with affinity audiences is worthwhile because they're huge and can be powerful, but it's not easy to profitably target window-shoppers. So I advise you to create an attention-grabbing video ad and then follow up with a video-and-website remarketing campaign.

CUSTOM AFFINITY-AUDIENCE TARGETING

What tends to work better than delegating the choice of affinity groups to Google is to build your own affinity audience *based on* Google's data. You can get Google to build you audiences—of more than one billion people in some cases—from people who, say, type in certain keywords and visit certain videos or websites.

Start small. Although custom affinity audiences can give you huge reach, like any affinity audience, they can also quickly bust your budget. You can spend many thousands of dollars a day on them, so test with small daily budgets to begin with. These audiences are tough to crack, but when you have figured them out, you will have built a huge audience with huge scaling opportunities.

IN-MARKET AUDIENCE TARGETING

Here's still another great targeting option to test for your business—Google group users who are researching products and actively considering buying a service or product that is similar to yours. For example, if I were researching a vacation and looking for flights, hotels, car rentals, etc., Google would track this and group me into a specific in-market audience such as "Travel" or substitute in-market audiences such as "Air Travel" or even "Air Travel by Class," "Cruises," or "Hotels & Accommodation."

In-market audiences are specially designed for advertisers focused on getting in front of in-store and checkout shoppers. As another example, if I were looking to sell a new line of luxury travel luggage, I would target in-market audiences including "Luggage," and in my demographic targeting, I would probably select a higher household income. Because I'm likely targeting checkout shoppers, I would also run a video ad that speaks directly to them.

With all these different options, it's not easy to translate the targeting choice to the customer's psychology or where they are in the buying cycle. Therefore, I have included an image below that shows what type of shopper you will be getting in front of when you choose certain targeting options:

THE SEQUENCE OF AD CAMPAIGNS: A BEGINNER'S GUIDE TO BUILDING YOUR FIRST CAMPAIGN

When you've considered appropriate targeting options and are ready to take action on creating videos, strategically choose your next steps. The act of throwing just anything at the YouTube wall and hoping it'll stick brings three risks: loss of time, loss of money, and loss of faith in YouTube. Follow my suggestions to get early wins that will encourage you to leverage more of what the platform can do for your business.

To recap the lessons to this point, find a moment and create an ad for one person in that moment, including a strong offer. Start with one type of campaign at a time, and master that one before moving on to the next. No book can explain everything about building, optimizing, scaling, and expanding campaigns. You can walk through the entire process of building your first campaign step-by-step with the free online Viewability Mini Course I mentioned at the beginning of this chapter. It's available in the "book resources" section on www.viewability.co.uk.

A cautionary note is worth keeping in mind. As with any advertising, you might lose some money for the first month as you learn the best places and means to advertise. When you're advertising on YouTube for the first time—and you're doing it on your own—run the ad, learn from the results, and adjust as needed. Chalk up that expense to education that'll help you succeed soon. Again, though, to limit the cost of that education, cap your daily budget at first, and scale only slowly—and never before you know what is working.

COMING UP: *HOW* TO LEARN FROM THE RESULTS

Now that you've built your ad campaigns, how do you learn everything they have to teach so you can optimize your campaigns? In the next chapter, you'll discover what you need to know to measure success.

Mastering the Moment: Bringing It All Together, One Moment at a Time

So far, you've created your ad and maybe you're already running your first campaign. Now it's time to optimize, scale, and expand your campaign. To gain profit and reach, you need to know what's working, so you can scale it up, and what's not working, so you can turn it off. To do so, you must measure results.

HYPOTHESIZE AND TRACK MILESTONES

To figure out whether the offer—and any other component of the video—is working, map out what's most important for you to know, so you can track it. What you're mapping are the milestones on your customers' journey through your sales funnel.

Even before the ad runs, start with a broad hypothesis of what you expect to happen as a result of the ad. In general, you'll expect to get your ad in front of the right people, whom you expect to watch, click, and land on your web page. Then you'll expect them to take some sort of action. Specify that action; of course, it will depend on your product or service and your business strategy for the campaign.

Map out the milestones on the path you want your customers to take, starting with watching the YouTube ad. Then, no matter what your product or service, you probably want them to click on the link in the ad that takes them to your website. For example, if you're running a webinar, the next milestone to celebrate is if users register. Then you want them to actually attend the webinar, but that's not necessarily the end of the funnel. Now you want attendees to take the next step still, which might be buying a product or signing up to be a client.

You can also hypothesize how many people will watch your ad, what percentage will click on your website, and what percentage will continue on through your customer journey. Predict those numbers for each step in that journey.

Once you are up and running, you can compare your hypotheses with the actual data on the number of people reaching each milestone. Google Analytics, a free online web tool, lets you track everything your viewers are doing, from the moment they see your ad through the moment they become customers. It will tell you exactly how each of your ads and targeting options is performing for you.

There's no excuse for not using this valuable tool.[1] If you need help creating and using your Google Analytics account, watch our video in the "book resources" section on www.viewability.co.uk.

MANY HAPPY—AND *SPEEDY*—RETURNS

Once you're measuring everything, you'll start to spot some winners—options for which you're earning two or more dollars for every dollar you spend. At that point, you'll want to scale as quickly as possible. Let ad cash flow determine your scaling speed.

Depending on what you're selling, you might know as soon as forty-eight hours whether a campaign works. You can expect an ad for a webinar to produce speedier returns than an ad for a car purchase. In the case of the car, though, viewers with interest in a test-drive might not book it or take it for a month or more. Once they test the car, they might take another couple of months to decide to buy it.

---

1   John Wanamaker, an American merchant and marketing pioneer, would have embraced Google Analytics. More than a century ago, he famously complained, "Half the money I spend on advertising is wasted; the trouble is, I don't know which half."

Instead of impatiently waiting to scale in that case, I recommend that you offer something—early in the sales funnel—that allows you to recoup the cost of advertising. Make it something attractive yet small in relation to the final purchase. If, for instance, you're selling expensive sports cars, that "beginner" sale could look like this: You could provide the option of *buying* the VIP experience of test-driving the car on a race track, rather than driving it near the dealership for free. When people book the paid option, four things happen:

- You get ROI on the day you run the ads, which lets you scale right away.
- You create a unique experience that appeals to the audience, so you're building a great relationship with the brand.
- People are far more likely to show up for and value a test-drive they paid for than one that came free.
- Paying for something also "qualifies" the person as a serious prospect who is ready to take action, so you're not wasting time and energy on the other type.

Our agency learned this lesson the hard way. In our ads to bring in new customers, we used to offer a free phone conversation. We spent a lot of time with people who ultimately weren't right for our agency. Now any prospect must start by paying for an audit of their campaigns or a strategy discussion of how YouTube can work for their business, which has worked well for us, our prospects, and our clients.

Any type of business can find an appropriate way to get speedier ROI—you just need to think about what your customers want and get creative. For example, a travel agent could charge a (maybe one-hundred-dollar) premium for a hands-off VIP experience—including customized activity arrangements. Perhaps the agent would visit your home at a time to suit you and your family, so you could all plan the perfect vacation together. I know I would happily pay more than one hundred dollars for that VIP service.

DEEP ANALYSIS

Once you start running your ad, the AdWords platform will generate a lot of data. Be patient with yourself because it can take some time to get used to what you're seeing. Don't let it scare you, though. You can't delete or destroy anything. You'll start to notice patterns that can give you useful insights into future actions.

We ran an ad for a client who helps people become better public speakers. When we checked the data, we found good results from the expected search keywords and video placements, but also meditation videos, which our targeting options kind of stumbled across. Our subsequent exploration showed us that some of the most successful businesspeople meditate. We used that insight to do more than target meditation videos; we actually created a video that reinforces the connection between meditation and public speaking. The results were even more dramatic.

SPLIT TEST AND TWEAK

I've filled this book and the accompanying resources on viewability.co.uk with best practices—techniques that our agency knows will work week in and week out because we've tested them. Still, it's unlikely that your campaign will hit it out of the park from day one. Measure and test everything to keep improving. I can't emphasize enough the value of measuring, testing, and optimizing.

Split testing can have a profound impact on results in situations where it's hard to know which of two angles will work better for the audience. It's not uncommon to see one ad outperform another by a very large margin. In a recent test, we ran several similar video ads with different sales angles, and one of the video ads was seventeen times more effective than another. We wouldn't have been able to predict this prior to running the ads, so it doesn't pay to run one at a time and hope for the best.

Split testing can help you improve not only your video ads, but also every milestone along the customer journey: the landing page, offer, product—everything. In our agency, for example, we've tested many variations on the question that greets visitors on our landing page to arrive at the most effective one: "Will YouTube ads work for you?" When you ride the winner in a split test, you compound the profitable effects of every bump in responses every day you run the ad, and advertising becomes so much easier.

NOW BREAK GROUND

Although asking questions, listening to customers' answers, and interpreting the data are essential, innovation often depends on shifting your thinking beyond what your customers and the data can tell you. As the apocryphal story goes, if Henry Ford had asked people what they wanted, they might have responded only with "a faster horse."

A widely distributed and affordable motorized solution didn't exist yet, so people couldn't think in those terms. Instead, of course, Ford used his knowledge of the market to visualize a new way to grant the wish for speed, both in travel and in assembly-line production.

The same type of visionary thinking has led to the first smartphone, then the smartwatch, and many other innovations we enjoy today. When customers can't directly help you find that innovation, try this method to begin to tap into the inventor's vision for your own business:

Ask yourself questions, such as "What could make my customer's life incredible?" and "What would it look like?" Empathize and focus on what customers would want. Also look to other industries to inspire you, as I've been encouraging with examples throughout this book in general, and this section in particular.

When you come up with ideas, avoid making them precious. Listen to people's reactions, but also use your judgment—give your ideas a chance. Take a page from the book of improvisational actors and watch your language: At the end of every sentence that discusses your idea, let the thought continue by adding "yes, and..." before continuing, and don't use the word "no."

Some people refer to innovation as a spark of brilliance. It is, but everyone can do it. You engineer it by asking the right questions of yourself and by being patient.

PREPARING FOR ACTION AND A WRAP

On your journey through this book so far, you've mapped your customer's moments and chosen one moment. You've created a video ad around that moment, and you've learned how to build profitable campaigns. Only one step remains, but it's a big one. The final chapter will go through some last-minute checks before you adventure into the world of YouTube advertising.

Momentum: The Adventure Starts Now

You've come a long way in this book. My sincere hope is that it has helped you to focus on your customers as never before—because you now know that's the key to success—*and* to lead with their one moment. I hope you've prepared an empathetic message for that moment, chosen an appealing offer, and learned how to build campaigns that test that appeal on YouTube. I also hope you believe in the many ways YouTube can deliver ROI and help you expand your business.

The best way to reinforce any learning is to (continue to) put it into practice. That may be especially true in the case of this learning, because—if you'll forgive my borrowing a line from TV and radio promotion—"you've got to be in it to win it." Nothing persuades like results, you can get them only when you advertise, and you can get more of them by following the advice in this book.

Before you rush off and start building, let's quickly review.

WHY YOUR BUSINESS NEEDS YOU TO FIND MOMENTS

1. MOMENTS BUILD PROFITS

With any type of advertising, the priority should always be on return on investment. But profits *and* brand building do not need to be mutually exclusive. Clients come to realize that ads that give their users an amazing user experience generate profits and build their brand.

2. MOMENTS BUILD *BRANDS*

When you pay attention to building your brand, you invest in your business's longevity. What supports both brands and profits is building a *relationship*, and that requires empathy and class. Demanding that customers "buy our stuff now!" may grab short-term sales, but it does very little for the brand.

Instead, people who view your videos should get to know, like, and trust you. They should bond with you and positively remember the experience. A good user experience alone invests in the future of your business. In the vast majority of cases, the best way to sell to a YouTube user is to provide an experience that elicits a reaction, such as "Wow, that was cool. What's next?!"

MOMENTS CONTRIBUTE TO A CIVIL SOCIETY

While you're taking care of business, also consider your responsibility both as an advertiser and as a citizen of the world. We all need to look at how we advertise in terms of the sort of society we want to inhabit. By providing positive experiences, we serve both responsibilities.

Annoying ads, on the other hand, change our experience of the internet for the worst. When people visit a platform that bombards them with useless ads, they're less likely to return. Those ads and subsequent desertions have often been a large contributing factor in the platform's death. That's no concern to the bombardier advertisers who take the money and run to destroy the next platform. But that attitude ultimately defeats the user (and we're all also users), YouTube, Google, and our collective view of the world.

Our duty to elevate the ad environment shares some aspects with the need to preserve the natural one. We know that if we continue to burn the Earth's fossil fuels at our current rate, we'll ruin our home. Of course, our obligation to save the Earth's ecosystem is far more critical than our obligation to save YouTube's. But YouTube's is the one that you might be better able to influence. Both preservation imperatives start with a similar thought process: "What can we do to take responsibility for our behavior and contribute to a more helpful environment?" We need to up our game and focus on *giving* value, not just taking.

GIVING AND RECEIVING EVERGREEN VALUE

The natural and ad environments also happen to share a word: Evergreen ad campaigns, like the tree they're named for, have timeless appeal. I recommend that you start with this type, rather than launching a campaign with a limited promotional period.

The benefit of keeping up the same ad—for a core product or service of your business—is that you can use what you learn over time to improve and scale it. In the first two weeks of the first month your ad runs, you might lose money, but you'll gain tracked data you can use to tweak the campaign. By the second half of the month, you should start to see results and break even. The longer the ad can run, the more it will show you how to hone it, and the more you will sell.

Eventually, the ad might need no more than an occasional tweak. When you finish optimizing and scaling, you'll have a profit tap that's always running, constantly selling for you. Now, you might be wondering whether people will get bored with the same ad. That's a "no" because, for one thing, thanks to Google, you're providing information for your users only when they need it. For another, you won't let them see any ad more than once. Once they click, you'll exert complete control over the experience: what viewers see and when, including your follow-up videos.

STRUGGLING? PLAN ADS FOR A BUSINESS THAT ISN'T YOURS

If you've reached this point in the book and have struggled to find a moment, a message, or an offer for your customer, you're probably experiencing what this old saying describes so aptly: "You can't read the label when you're inside the jar." Right—you're too close to your business to have the perspective you need to leap the hurdles we tend to put in our own way.

In that case, you'll probably find it valuable to start by going through the process for someone else's company. Having begun with someone else's, you're better able to see beyond limitations that might have stopped you before. Once you get the hang of that, you may see the way to your own solution.

You'll also release pressure, sharpen your focus, and maybe even have fun if you invite your friends and colleagues to join you in the exercise. For different perspectives, gather people of different demographics and backgrounds—marketers and non-marketers alike. For example, my wife, a non-marketer, often lends a valuable perspective I never would have found on my own. Attempting a creative process with only experts in the room can result in narrow, headstrong thinking. Even if outside participants get it wrong, that experience can help to determine what "it" is.

FINAL CHECKS: WILL IT FLY?

Before you go live with your ad, take a clear-eyed look at it. Remember, we're not holding out for perfection; don't let anxiety stand in the way of going live, because there's *always* some uncertainty until you get in front of your audience. But do look at the ad from the perspective of your audience—and an airplane.

I borrowed the latter idea from my psychology studies. Imagine yourself in a plane looking at your campaign 30,000 feet below: Does it fit you and YouTube? Is it the right offer for this person's moment? Does it look good? You'll also be wise to bring other passengers on your flight and welcome any feedback.

Now descend to 15,000 feet, where you and your companions can see more details and the script (assuming you have really good eyes): Does it sound authentic? Have you made the offer easy to accept? Keep descending to see more detail through your audience's eyes until you're satisfied with your campaign on the ground.

Take stock and make sure you feel comfortable before you go live with your ads. If, after you go live, it turns out you've been seeing your ad and others' feedback through tinted glasses, you'll receive the most brutal feedback of all: adding up what you spent to find out your ad doesn't work. Learn to spot major problems early, before they cost you—before you go live with any ad.

At the same time, please avoid the common traps of perfectionism, self-doubt, and procrastination. Begin to run the ad as soon as you receive—and act on—the best advice you can get. You'll learn a huge amount from the experience that you can use to fine-tune your first campaign and to build a better second one. If you never go live, you'll never know. *Nothing* is more effective than testing in the actual marketplace. So, when you're satisfied, go live and try not to panic—too much.

WHAT TO EXPECT IN THE FIRST FEW DAYS OF GOING LIVE

Video-ad-campaign panic is remarkably common. When people post their first campaign, they tend to hit the refresh button every few minutes. They want every bit of data in real time, which is not only useless, it's also crazy making. In the words of one of my clients, "If I had a dollar for every time I refreshed my campaigns to check stats, I'd generate a million dollars every night."

In fact, this type of panic is so common that we thought of making fun of it with a video showing a business owner doing parkour (flips and leaps up and across buildings) to speed across town to get to his computer: "Okay, it's been two whole minutes. Get me a stat update."

Panic and its first cousin, excitement, often arise from the stories that go around about claims of overnight internet-ad millionaires. Ninety-nine percent of the time, they're false. We've made people a lot of money, but it takes our hard work, time, and expertise to get there; it rarely happens overnight. Even if you do see a load of sales in the first day, realize that more went into those results than just the last twenty-four hours of promotion. I think it's irresponsible for marketing consultants to suggest otherwise.

The worst part about panicking is it can drive people to make premature changes, which resets the whole algorithm and can provide confusing results. You've got to let a campaign breathe: Unless you notice runaway ad expense with no conversions, let it do its thing for forty-eight to seventy-two hours—up to a week. Don't spend more than you can afford, and be okay with the fact that you'll probably lose some "research money" at first.

Whether you panic or not, be prepared for fluctuations. Some things may not work, so you'll turn them off—leaving you with only winning targeting options and videos. But *then*, you might watch results slowly die off, and you'll have no good explanation for their death. These fluctuations are typical enough that they have names. When you release your first video, you enter the "honeymoon" phase: Nobody has seen your brand before, so everyone interacts with it, partly out of curiosity. From there, you move into a "consistent" phase—the numbers hold for a time. Finally, if things are going well enough that you can scale up, you may experience a "fatigue" phase, in which sales drop off because every likely prospect has seen your ads several times. This is the time to replace your video ads.

You might never experience a fatigue phase, though, because you have our methodology, so your ads should always be relevant and useful to your users. They should appear only when your users are looking for you in their moment of need.

OPTIMIZE AND SCALE

After that critical first forty-eight to seventy-two hours when you've seen what's consistently working and what isn't, you can move on to optimizing. Hit the "pause" button on anything that isn't doing its job (such as the wrong keyword or a placement campaign that costs more than it gives) and run the ad for another week.

Things should look up in the second week. First, because you've paused aspects that didn't work, this week's advertising will cost less than that of the first one. You might even see a profit, even though the pauses result in lower volume. You could run that profitable ad forever, or you could scale in the next week, in one of three ways:

- Boost your budget across campaigns.
- Boost your budget per view.
- Find new avenues. Use data analysis to inform your next steps. See where you've received good results and look for trends you can capitalize upon. This is how we were able to notice that our client's public-speaking-training ads did extraordinarily well when they showed on videos about meditation. When we created video ads that "met this moment," the results got even stronger.

RINSE AND REPEAT

When you've followed one moment through its ad campaign and garnered results and knowledge, restart the build-optimize-scale process for another moment, then another, until you've captured them all. Your core audience might include five or six types of customers, but the moments and customers you explore don't need to differ sharply from the ones your first ad targeted. You can learn a lot from even slight variations.

For example, I'm recalling a cosmetics ad where we

targeted thirty-five- to fifty-five-year-old women. Our research told us that the cosmetic wish list of women who are thirty-five to forty-five varies somewhat from those forty-five to fifty-five, so we used different ads for each age bracket. We arrived at that strategy by thinking about how to be most helpful and layering that thinking onto the research.

On the other hand, if you spend too much time on tweaking, you might see diminishing returns. When one moment is working well, move on to the next one—maybe even a new moment each week. You might get comfortable enough to test five moments at once, but I recommend that you resist the temptation to rush. To avoid costly errors, heed the familiar advice applied here to ad activity: "Crawl before you walk and walk before you run." Remembering why you're advertising—to build brands and make money for your business—will help you take the long view.

Of course, we've got an agency that can help you get results with your ads. With this book and the web training and tools you can access with it, though, you can accomplish a lot on your own.

Then move beyond this book. I hope you'll find your own way, choose your own adventure, and develop your own brand. Even if you ultimately decide to work with us, you'll be a better partner because you'll know more about the process than if you had started from scratch.

Also, feel free to prove me wrong about any of the lessons in this book. Like any ad campaign, this book is a work in progress. Our agency tests the book's lessons day in and day out, so we know they're valuable. But building an ad campaign is science mixed with art. The science evolves, as campaigns, technology, and people do, which is why this book has given you this scientific approach:

- Build out some campaigns and try things out.
- Optimize the campaigns by turning off anything that isn't working.
- Scale up what is working.
- Expand upon your success by using your data to build a new campaign.

As you've seen throughout this book, the process really begins by starting and *empathizing* with the user. Empathy will always lead you to your customers. It will also lead you to the point where you can say, "I'm ready to get started. Based on what I know right now, this is the best decision I can make." Rather than thinking of the book as prescriptive, consider it your springboard to advertising on YouTube. See where it takes you, and where your creativity can take you next.

YOUR ADVENTURE STARTS NOW

We've talked a lot about moments in this book, and I have two more to mention. The first is the whole reason I wrote this book for you. If you apply what I have taught you here and work hard at crafting this amazingly powerful skill, you will reach a moment in the next week or so in which you record your first profitable day. You can do this, and this moment will change your life. You will have created a reliable and repeatable system in which you put a dollar in and get more than a dollar out. What's more, while you're making a profit, you're also serving your customers and building a powerhouse brand. My first experience with this moment was brilliantly empowering; it was then that I realized I was in control of my future and could start realizing my dreams. I want you to experience this moment, too.

The second moment is happening right now. You've read this far, which is awesome, but now you need to take action. Too often people learn but don't do. This is your moment to make sure you do. See you on YouTube.

GOT THE BOOK? GET THE COURSE AND MORE

To further help you on your journey, visit the "book resources" page at Viewability.co.uk for free video courses and more helpful tools for successful YouTube advertising.

About the Author

 **TOM BREEZE** is founder and CEO of Viewability, a company specializing in YouTube advertising, boasting an impressive client list of international brands. With a "Pay for Results" financial model, Viewability and partners are now the highest-spending performance-based YouTube advertising company worldwide. Tom is also a speaker and consultant, teaching businesses around the world how to advertise successfully on YouTube.